SERMONS FROM THE MOUNT

Sermons
From the Mount

CHARLES M. CROWE

ABINGDON PRESS

New York • *Nashville*

SERMONS FROM THE MOUNT

Copyright MCMLIV by Pierce & Washabaugh

Library of Congress Catalog Card Number: 54-5941

3

SET UP, PRINTED, AND BOUND BY THE
PARTHENON PRESS, AT NASHVILLE,
TENNESSEE, UNITED STATES OF AMERICA

DEDICATED
to the memory of
THE MATER

"Could we but put in practice the Sermon on the Mount, all the problems of our poor tortured universe would be solved, all the difficulties, apparently insuperable, which confront mankind would melt like the mist before the rising sun."

—A. J. Cronin, *Adventures in Two Worlds*

CONTENTS

"And seeing the multitudes, he went up into a mountain: and when he was set, his disciples came unto him: and he opened his mouth, and taught them, saying, Blessed are the poor in spirit: for their's is the kingdom of heaven. Blessed are they that mourn: for they shall be comforted. Blessed are the meek: for they shall inherit the earth. Blessed are they which do hunger and thirst after righteousness: for they shall be filled. Blessed are the merciful: for they shall obtain mercy. Blessed are the pure in heart: for they shall see God. Blessed are the peacemakers: for they shall be called the children of God. Blessed are they which are persecuted for righteousness' sake: for their's is the kingdom of heaven. Blessed are ye, when men shall revile you, and persecute you, and shall say all manner of evil against you falsely, for my sake. Rejoice, and be exceeding glad: for great is your reward in heaven: for so persecuted they the prophets which were before you."

—*Matthew 5:1-12*

THE JOYOUS LIFE

Blessed are the poor in spirit:
for their's is the kingdom of heaven.

IN the year 1921 Lyman Abbott was seated in a pastor's study. His book *What Christianity Means to Me* had just been published, and he was waiting to review it before an audience in the church. The pastor asked Dr. Abbott to autograph his personal copy of the book. "Write in it," the pastor said, "the ripest thought that has come into your mind during your sixty years of Christian growth." Dr. Abbott took out his fountain pen and sat down to write. The pastor left the room at that point. About thirty minutes later the pastor returned. Dr. Abbott had not written a word. He was deep in thought. Returning some time later to take the speaker to the meeting, the pastor found the book open with this sentence on the flyleaf with the ink scarcely dry: *"The Christianity of Jesus was not a philosophy which he taught; it is a life which he imparts."*

This observation may well be a key to our understanding of the Sermon on the Mount. In it Jesus does not set up some detailed doctrine for human thinking nor a definite plan for conduct. He seeks to impart a divine, human quality of life that is different from the earthy ordinary. The Sermon is a message designed to make life winsome, brave, free, and full. Behind this message of the Master is the life of the Master. They go together. To understand his message, we must know him. Out from his mind and spirit comes a life-changing message of divine beauty, strength, power, and hope.

It is significant that the Sermon begins with the note of joy. Jesus used the word "blessed" or "happy" to introduce each of the nine Beatitudes. They deserve to be treated separately. But in dealing with them as a unit, we may take the first one as a summary of them all. "Blessed are the poor in spirit: for their's is the kingdom of heaven." For to be in the kingdom, as has been said, *is* to be comforted, to inherit the earth, to be satisfied, to obtain mercy, to see God, and to be called his sons. The Beatitudes thus reveal a secret of human happiness contrary to the usual and accepted ideas on the subject. The joyous life of which Jesus speaks is the outgrowth of inner serenity and strength. It is a by-product of a life that is lived with God.

The Beatitudes introduce us to at least three aspects of the joyous life which are also clues to its attainment.

I

The Beatitudes *emphasize the importance of happiness in Christian experience*. Dr. L. P. Jacks, a British theologian, said:

Christianity is the most encouraging, the most joyous, the least repressive, and the least forbidding of all the religions of mankind. There is no religion which throws off the burden of life so completely, which escapes so swiftly from sad moods, which gives so large a scope for the high spirits of the soul, and welcomes to its bosom with so warm an embrace those things of beauty which are a joy forever.

"Blessed . . . blessed . . . blessed." "Happy . . . happy . . . happy." This is the one thought common to all the Beatitudes. Nine times in nine verses Jesus drove home this idea, climaxing it with a "punch line," *"Rejoice, and be exceeding glad."* It was for him no superficial or passing notion. It was an integral part of his own life and message. The note of the New Testament from beginning to end is one of triumphant joy. It begins with the singing of angels and ends with rejoicing around the throne of God. The gospel itself means "good news." The Master's typical greeting was, "Be of good cheer." In fact, as someone has pointed out, he gave us "three cheers." First, the cheer of forgiveness: "Be of good cheer; thy sins be forgiven thee." Second, the cheer of companionship: "Be of good cheer; it is I; be not afraid." Third, the cheer of victory: "Be of good cheer; I have overcome the world." Furthermore, he said that he wanted his joy to remain with us that our joy might be full.

This sense of quiet, exalted, uplifting joy is largely lacking on the modern Christian scene. Philosophers and scientists have filled our minds with gloomy forebodings. Psychiatry has exposed and dwelt on the animal and ugly side of human nature.

Many Christian teachers have retreated into a religion of crisis, pessimism, negation, and helplessness. Our world depresses us with terrifying events. The nagging fears and pressures of every day keep our spirits at low level.

. There is an interesting index of the effect of all this on our bodies and personalities. The production of sleeping pills has multiplied four times in twenty years! A staggering mountain of 350 tons of these barbiturates is manufactured each year in the United States. This is enough to put everyone in the country to sleep for 22 nights a year—or enough to put nine million people to sleep for 365 nights a year. When the awakening pills are added in, the total comes to more than 5,500,000,000 doses annually in this country.

Is life so unhappy, so desperate, so grim, that even normal people must resort to drugs to blot it out? Are sleeping pills to be a monument to our miserable lot? It takes more than barbiturates to overcome the world. We need the renewal of a sane and solid faith that expresses itself in serenity and joy. The joyous life is a cure for many of our worries and mental roadblocks. It helps us maintain healthy minds and bodies. A joyous life makes it easier for us to get along with other people. It contributes to our mental balance and to a healthy attitude toward life. It builds a margin of safety around our souls.

Burnett H. Streeter said one time, "In his actual teaching, Christ speaks as if he conceived conduct as the art of life—an art of solid building, yet with something of the dancer's gaiety." We must recover the gaiety at the heart of our faith! Otherwise we misrepresent the Master and his message. The Christian life is the joyous life. Too long have we Christians walked with downcast eyes and burdened hearts. We have talked much of Christian sacrifice and service and love. We need to exhibit more Christian joy. We are the redeemed of God! Our faith is not

12

dominated by somber tones or dark moods. It is glorified by a blessed lightness of heart. Our songs are as weapons against our enemies. Our cheerful poise marks us as whole personalities, sons of God.

II

The Beatitudes *state the conditions of a joyous life*. The blessedness of which Jesus spoke is no surface matter. It is certainly no back-slapping, pleasure-seeking frivolity. Neither is it a cheap affectation to be turned on and off at will. It is rather the normal expression of a dedicated life. Who are the happy ones? Not necessarily the rich, the aggressive, the privileged, the educated, the successful, the proud, the healthy. Rather, said Jesus, they are those who are humble of spirit, who are seekers after righteousness, who are gentle, understanding, and forgiving, who are pure in heart and makers of peace, who are steadfast in the face of evil opposition. To these, happiness comes naturally and unawares, without formula or fuss or fanfare. We don't go out and find happiness. It finds us when we fulfill the conditions.

These conditions set forth in the Beatitudes are uniquely interpreted by Fulton Oursler, in his book *The Precious Secret*, as eight rules for mental health and happiness. "Poor in spirit" becomes *We will never be content with anything that we do*. In other words, we will always be seekers, for arrogance and conceit and smug, self-satisfied complacency make happiness impossible. "They that mourn" becomes *We know that in grief we can grow strong*. Dedicated sorrow is an open door to new experiences of strength and joy. The reference to "the meek" becomes *We will accept misfortune in good faith*. That is to say, happiness comes neither by submission nor by rebellion before the rough events of life, but by our acceptance and use of these things. Meekness is not weakness. It is the recognition that life is governed by wise and just laws and includes a willingness to co-operate with these laws.

In Fulton Oursler's interpretations the phrase "They which do hunger and thirst after righteousness" is said to mean *We will have an unquenchable interest in knowledge and truth.* "It is the happy man's joy to acquire knowledge and to seek wisdom, sure path to the ancient ideal of righteousness. . . . Happy people are never satisfied with what they know, but are endlessly seeking more from the mystery of life." The fifth Beatitude, "Blessed are the merciful," is put into these words: *We will keep clean of grudges.* Hate and anger tend to cause diseases of mind and body. When we persist in feelings of bitterness, envy, and jealousy toward others, we are merely forcing unhappiness on ourselves. The happy man is he who overlooks little slights and forgives larger offenses.

"The pure in heart." What does this mean? *We will have a goal and pursue it faithfully.* Singlehearted attachment to some worthy work or some lofty purpose is pureness of heart and brings happiness. Achievements do not matter as much as goals. When our heart is in our work and when that work is big enough to give to it all that we are and have, then we discover joy and peace, almost without knowing it. "Blessed are the peacemakers." These are those who follow this rule: *We will do more than we are required to do.* The happy person never lives just for himself. He does and gives more than his duty. Deep, personal satisfactions come to those who serve others who may need the ministry of God's peace.

The eighth and ninth Beatitudes belong together. What is to be said for those who are persecuted and reviled? *We will learn the true values of obstacles and even of viciously unfair treatment.* In other words, even injustice and persecution have a constructive value. Happy is the person who is not crushed by them, but who rises above them. He is greater than his persecutors and is always victor.

Interpret them as we will, these are the conditions of the joyous life. They are conditions that may be met by any man, regardless of circumstances. For human happiness is determined not by what goes on outside, but by what goes on inside.

III

The Beatitudes *describe the results that come to those who meet the conditions of the joyous life.* Happiness is not an end in itself. Why be humble of spirit? Why hunger and thirst after righteousness? Why be merciful and pure in heart? Just to be happy? Not at all. We are happy as we do these things because the doing of them brings us into a true and active fellowship with God. These Beatitudes are not merely psychological principles. They are religious ideals. "For their's is the kingdom of heaven." "For they shall see God." "For they shall be called the children of God." "For great is your reward in heaven." Other and more detailed results, nonetheless divine, are promised. Those who grieve shall be comforted. Those who are meek—that is, who show good will toward men and reverent obedience toward God (which is the meaning of the Greek word)—shall inherit the earth. Those who show mercy will get it; and those who search after goodness will find it.

These are rewards worth having. They exalt human life and make it great. They do not come to the sad-eyed or the weak-kneed, nor to the wishful thinkers or the lightheaded. Neither do they come to the proud, the aggressive, the covetous, the vulgar, or to the compromisers. They are, however, the normal possession of those who live actively within the divine dimensions of life.

All this means that the joyous life is not a matter of whistling in the dark. It is, rather, true fulfillment for the child of God. The joyous life is not bounded by our environment nor dependent on the achievements of our heart's desires. It is, rather, the discovery that the universe is on our side and that we are a part of that unnumbered host of the fellowship of the Kingdom. It comes to those who see behind the seen the unseen meaning of life. This is to share in the ultimate purposes of the eternal God.

Such things are beyond understanding to the materialist, the pleasure hound, the go-getter, the cynic, the practical success-worshiper. But to those who live by and for the truth of God, nothing else has meaning at all.

Tycho Brahe was a brilliant young astronomer of Denmark. King Frederick had built for him an observatory on a little island. Tycho called it Uraniborg, "the City of the Heavens." There he worked day and night for many years, charting the stars with great precision. Then the king died. His successor looked with disfavor on Tycho's work at Uraniborg and begrudged the money it required. He sent his messengers to inquire of the astronomer what he had been doing these twenty-five years and how he could justify his budget. They laughed at him when he told them he had charted seven hundred stars and hoped to have charted a thousand before he died. Then they asked him what practical use his work had for the people of Denmark in that time.

Here is Tycho's answer in the poem *The Watchers of the Sky* by Alfred Noyes:

> "In the time to come,"
> Said Tycho Brahe, "perhaps a hundred years,
> Perhaps a thousand, when our own poor names
> Are quite forgotten, and our kingdoms dust,
> On one sure certain day, the torch-bearers

Will, at some point of contact, see a light
Moving upon this chaos. Though our eyes
Be shut forever in an iron sleep,
Their eyes shall see the kingdom of the law,
Our undiscovered cosmos. They shall see it,—
A new creation rising from the deep,
Beautiful, whole.
       We are like men that hear
Disjointed notes of some supernal choir.
Year after year, we patiently record
All we can gather. In that far-off time,
A people that we have not known shall hear them,
Moving like music to a single end."

The worldly-minded messengers could not understand such
talk. They never do. They reported to the king that Tycho
Brahe's dreams were fruitless and perilous. So Tycho went out
to exile, and Uraniborg went into the dust. Yet said Tycho:

We are on the verge of great discoveries.
I feel them as a dreamer feels the dawn
Before his eyes are opened. Many of you
Will see them. In that day you will recall
This, our last meeting at Uraniborg,
And how I told you that this work of ours
Would lead to victories for the coming age.
The victors may forget us. What of that?
Theirs be the palms, the shouting, and the praise.
Ours be the father's glory in the sons.[1]

The Tycho Brahes are the happy people. For those who live in
the spirit of God find God. To expend oneself as Tycho did for
some unreachable and noble ideal—this is close to the heart of

[1] Copyright 1922, 1949, by Alfred Noyes. From *The Torch Bearers*. Used
by permission of the author and the publishers, J. B. Lippincott Co. and
William Blackwood & Sons, Ltd.

religion. To be partners with God in the creation of his king-dom—this is reward enough for any man. It is a cure for our discontent and our weariness. It is the open door to those deeper satisfactions of the soul which alone undergird our peace and bring us life that is joyous and blessed beyond understanding. When we are committed without reserve to God's eternal pur-poses, no failure can defeat us, and our joy is complete and secure.

CHAPTER TWO

"Ye are the salt of the earth: but if the salt have lost his savour, wherewith shall it be salted? it is thenceforth good for nothing, but to be cast out, and to be trodden under foot of men. Ye are the light of the world. A city that is set on an hill cannot be hid. Neither do men light a candle, and put it under a bushel, but on a candlestick; and it giveth light unto all that are in the house. Let your light so shine before men, that they may see your good works, and glorify your Father which is in heaven." —Matthew 5:13-16

THE RADIANT LIFE

Let your light so shine.

WE all know something of the wonderful way in which light is used in our modern world. We have invisible black light and infrared light. We have watch dials that glow in the dark. We have indirect lighting of rooms. We have X-ray light that enables us to see through many solid objects. Then there is a new and different development in this field of lighting. It is the use of light to test how well a machine is operating. The Kodak Research Laboratories have made powders of varicolored phosphorus. These powders glow differently at different temperatures. When they are coated on a cool object, the powders shine brightly. When the object gets warmer, they darken. For instance, the parts of a moive machine may be coated with this powder. Should the machine get overheated with it is running, the glowing powder will lose its brilliance at that point. In this

19

way engineers can find weak spots in many things, from ship turbines to airplane wings.

It is interesting to know that Jesus applied this same test of light to the life of men two thousand years ago. "Ye are the light of the world. A city that is set on an hill cannot be hid. Neither do men light a candle, and put it under a bushel, but on a candlestick; and it giveth light unto all that are in the house. Let your light so shine before men, that they may see your good works, and glorify your Father which is in heaven." Jesus seems to be saying that God has given us the ability to glow, to radiate light, to shine. He is encouraging us to let this luminous quality of life have a chance. He warns us against hiding it, lest by so doing we will weaken our effectiveness as persons. In other words, Christians are to be lighted, shining personalities, thus unmistakably identifying themselves as belonging to the company of God's children.

This light test finds most of us sadly lacking these days. We Christians are too often likely to be dull, ordinary people. We often lose our brilliance at our weak spots. The angry fears and ugly events of life have been as bushel baskets hiding our glowing spirits. We need to recover the ability to shine—not in a cheap, superficial sense, but in a real, deep, Christian sense. Jesus himself was a radiant personality in the highest and best sense. In this passage he is telling us how we, too, may live the radiant, shining life.

I

Jesus is saying here that *we are important persons*. We like to think of important people as those who have famous and important names. Paul, Christopher Columbus, Martin Luther, Florence Nightingale, George Washington, Jane Addams, David Livingstone, Herbert Hoover. These are the important people, we say. However, Jesus talked on the Mount with people we never heard of. They were plain, everyday people whose names were not even recorded. Yet Jesus called these average people the light of the world! It was his way of telling them that they were important people, that they mattered in the sight of God and man. Jesus was always interested in getting people to think highly of themselves. For he knew they would never shine like lights unless they did.

Even if our names are not famous, they are nevertheless important to us. Our names represent us to the world. A name takes on the reputation of the person who bears it. Sometimes this can be carried to extremes. For instance, in the Domesday Book, the census made by William the Conqueror in England, there were English people by the name of Badneighbor, Blackinthemouth, Gotobed, and Losewit. On the early passenger lists of boats arriving at Plymouth, Massachusetts, there are such names as Lumphead, Styffchynn, and Inchbald! Good descriptive names, all!

We smile at these names and are glad we are not afflicted with them. But whatever our name is, it stands for something. It stands for us! If we are "cheapskates," our names reflect this idea. If we are fussy and ill-tempered, people think of this when our names are mentioned. If we are mean and dishonorable and dishonest, our names stand for this.

The point is that a good name is a valuable possession. It is worth working for. For instance, some growers of oranges paid $1,250,000 for the exclusive right to the trade name of their brand of oranges. It is an important trade name. The people who use it are very careful that their oranges are of the very best quality.

Well, the name "Christian" is worth much more than a million dollars. It is priceless. Anyone who bears the name Christian is marked as an important person. The very name carries a sacred trust. It makes us representative of Jesus Christ. The name Christian stands for faith in God as superior Ruler. The name Christian stands for character that is strong and clean and honorable. The name Christian stands for a spirit that is generous and courageous and kind. The name Christian stands for love and forgiveness and hope and truth. The name Christian stands for the right, true, and good things. These qualities make us stand up straight and give us faith in life and in ourselves. They make us shine like a light in a darkened world. The Christian, therefore, guards his name. He makes his name stand for something big and fine and holy. The Christian is the most important person in the world. When we say, "I am a Christian," we can hold our heads high and be proud of it. For no other name means so much.

II

Jesus is saying that *we should be attractive persons.* Some years ago a young lad wanted very much to be an actor. He did not, however, have much ability. Moreover, his mother was opposed to his going into the theater. At the age of nineteen he had his first small part in a play and for the first time walked on a stage. He was awkward and unattractive. In fact, people laughed at him, and his mother even hissed him. He was overcome by stage fright and left the stage in tears and humiliation. No one would have guessed that night that this boy was to become the greatest of American actors, Richard Mansfield.

What was responsible for this great change? It came about by hard work and painstaking training. His private secretary, Grenville Kleiser, said that Mr. Mansfield studied carefully every drama he played. In preparation he would spend hours rehearsing a single line in order to give it the truest interpretation. In this connection, Mansfield gave much time to cultivating his speaking voice to make it attractive. He said one time, "When you are enacting a part, think of your voice as a color and as you paint your picture (the scene you are portraying) mix your colors. You have on your palette a white voice . . . ; a heavenly ethereal, or blue voice, the voice of prayer; a disagreeable, jealous, or yellow voice; . . . a brown voice of hopelessness; a lurid red voice of hot rage; . . . a cheery voice, the color of the green sea, that a brisk breeze is crisping."

Well, in a sense all of us are actors in the human drama. The trouble is, so many of us never get beyond the awkward, childish stage. We go through life running from our fears and crying in humiliation over criticism, opposition, and obstacles. The brown voice of hopelessness and the red voice of anger drown out the other voices. We think it is smart to make fun of the simple virtues. We rely on cleverness instead of goodness. We let show pass for sincerity and bravado for bravery. We are all too often "ham" actors, bungling the meaning of our parts.

God intended us for more than this! We are to represent him in the dramatic theater that is the world. God has given all of us the native abilities to become great in our part, whatever it may be. We develop a matchless attractiveness as we earnestly study the role of the Christian. We have to work at the job of interpreting Jesus to the world! We work at other things; why not work at being a Christian? As we practice the Christian spirit and rehearse the Christian faith, our lives become radiant with the divine grace and appeal. And in our voices will be found the blue voice of prayer and the cheery voice of the green sea crisping in the wind.

One of the real Christians of our day who has played a great role on the world's stage is General Douglas MacArthur. Above his desk in Tokyo was a framed message which read in part as follows:

Years wrinkle the skin, but to give no enthusiasm, wrinkles the soul. Worry, doubt, self-distrust, fear and despair—these are the long, long years that bow the head and turn the growing spirit back to dust. Whether seventy or sixteen, there is in every being's heart the love of wonder, the sweet amazement of the stars and the starlike things and thoughts, the undaunted challenge of the events, the unfailing childlike appetite for what next, and the joy of the game of life. You are as young as your faith, as old as your doubt; as young as your self-confidence, as old as your fear; as young as your hope, as old as your despair.

These are the things that make life attractive and satisfying. They are the things of the spirit. The life of selfishness and hatred, of sin and disbelief, is the bitter, ugly, and forbidding life. It is not only wrong; it is repulsive! The life of the Christian is always the attractive and radiant life. "Let your light shine"! The Christian should be and can be the happiest, most appealing, most interesting, and most popular person in the world.

III

Jesus is saying that *we can be influential persons.* Scientists have found a new way to send voice and vision across the continent. It was first used at the Japanese peace treaty conference in San Francisco. When the President greeted the delegates, the people on the east coast saw and heard him by what is called radio relay. This new relay system makes use of a super-high-frequency radio beam called a microwave. The beam vibrates four million times per second. It bounds back and forth between relay towers spaced thirty miles apart. No cables or wires are used between these station towers. The waves go from one station to another. When the microwaves are picked up by one relay tower, they are given a ten-millionfold boost and sent on to the next station. And so across mountains and forests the messages travel over the nation.

Here, surely, is a parable of the radiant life. We Christians are the relay stations of the spirit! We can be relay towers by which the message and picture of Jesus Christ are sent on to others. We pick up the signal from someone else. In our own personalities we strengthen it and boost its power. Then, bright and shining, it travels on to our loved ones, our friends, our associates, and on across the world.

Here, surely, is a description of how the radiant life works. "Let your light so shine before men, that they may see your good works, and glorify your Father which is in heaven." The Christian does not just enjoy his religion. He puts it to work in quiet deeds of love and faith. His influence on others may be direct. The verse implies, however, that the most effective influence we exert is indirect. People know us for what we actually are, not from our false front of good behavior when we want to make a good impression. The radiant Christian always reflects the spirit of Jesus Christ in all its beauty and power. He is understanding and helpful and forgiving and thoughtful of the needs of his brother men. He is high in faith and low in criticism. He lets the light of Christ shine through. He stands out above the crowd. He is unmistakably different in his actions and attitudes. It is this factor more than our pious preachments that influences the world for Christ. Indeed, the kingdom of God comes by the station-to-station, person-to-person relay route.

Robert Browning wrote a beautiful poem called "Pippa Passes." In the poem the story is told of a murder and of the guilt that goes with it. The scene of this evil is a house by the road. It is a setting of passion and bitterness, vileness and violence. On a lovely summer morning the young girl Pippa passes this house of shame. She is a happy, lighthearted girl, and she sings because she is happy. She has no thought of doing good to anybody. She does not realize that anyone is listening. And yet her simple song of happiness floats through the casement window and becomes a ministry of healing and light to the tormented hearts inside the house.

So it is that the radiant life, without even knowing it, can often do more than reproach or condemnation to lift the lives of men. We never know how much good we do by just being a lighted personality. The serene soul and the singing heart move with winsome power upon doubting minds and weary spirits. Millions today need this ministry. They live in the shadow of sin and fear. They do not need arguments or blame. They need the encouragement and example of radiant lives. This is the high privilege of the Christian. We may not amount to much. Our own lives may have tasted defeat. But we can let shine through to others the influence of a triumphant and glowing soul. Such lives are lights along the way that guide us home to God.

CHAPTER THREE

"Think not that I am come to destroy the law, or the prophets: I am not come to destroy, but to fulfil. For verily I say unto you, Till heaven and earth pass, one jot or one tittle shall in no wise pass from the law, till all be fulfilled. Whosoever therefore shall break one of these least commandments, and shall teach men so, he shall be called the least in the kingdom of heaven: but whosoever shall do and teach them, the same shall be called great in the kingdom of heaven. For I say unto you, That except your righteousness shall exceed the righteousness of the scribes and Pharisees, ye shall in no case enter into the kingdom of heaven."

—Matthew 5:17-20

THE SUPERIOR LIFE

Except your righteousness shall exceed the righteousness of the scribes and Pharisees, ye shall in no
case enter into the kingdom.

ONE time R. H. L. Sheppard said, "Christianity consists not in abstaining from doing things no gentleman would think of doing, but in doing things that are unlikely to occur to anyone who is not in touch with the spirit of Christ."

These thirty-five words are a pointed exposition of the section of the Sermon on the Mount which is brought to a climax by our text. The religion that Jesus taught was far from a matter of simple moral decency. Conventional respectability was not enough for him. The scribes and Pharisees were honest, law-abiding people. They were above reproach so far as the morality of the day was concerned. But this was not what Jesus was talking about. He wanted his followers to show a superior kind

27

of morality, based on a vital relationship with God the Father. Righteousness for him was no negative thing. It was a positive, dynamic, spiritual attitude toward life.

Someone has found that there are fifty million people in the United States who cannot furnish legal proof that they were born. That is, their birth certificates are missing. Much more serious, however, is the fact that millions of people give no evidence *of any kind* that they are really alive. They are good but dull. It is before these that Jesus would lift the challenge of the superior life. He calls us to a kind of morality that is alive with power and beauty. It is goodness forgetful of self, magnified by love, purified through suffering, and glorified in dedication.

"Except your righteousness shall *exceed*." Suppose we consider some aspects of this superior life.

I

The Christian life demands *superior discipline*. The Christian is not satisfied with merely meeting the average requirements of the society in which he lives. He demands the best of himself. This is no easy matter. It requires purification of self. It requires a stern self-discipline which most of us do not like.

Luther Burbank held sometimes what his neighbors called $10,000 bonfires. Into such a bonfire there might go 499 cherry plants out of the 500 that he had grown. Or there might be 99,999 rose bushes which had been brought to bloom in order to find the one specimen which was saved from the fire. On one occasion 1,500 gladiolus bulbs were burned after a half dozen of the finest plants had been preserved. What was the secret of such a proceeding? Said Mr. Burbank, "It is better to run the risk of losing a perfected product, through the destruction of the elements that went into it, than to issue forth to the world a lot of second bests which will clutter the earth with inferiority or mediocrity." In others words, Luther Burbank insisted on nothing but the best. He was impatient of imperfection. It was no accident that he was called the "plant wizard"!

There is a striking parallel here for the Christian life. Jesus, too, held before men the counsels of perfection. "Be ye therefore perfect, even as your Father which is in heaven is perfect." "Except your righteousness shall exceed." When this superior idealism becomes our guide, a pruning process takes place. Christianity is more ethically demanding than most of us realize. When we set our faces toward godlikeness, we turn away from those habits and attitudes that are inferior and godless. We can't serve both God and the Devil at the same time.

Many of us are second-rate people and second-rate Christians because we have been satisfied with second-rate living. We want to be good and be bad at the same time. There are too many middle-of-the-road Christians who have never dared some glorious Christian vision. There are too many average, ordinary Christians who are easily satisfied with some pleasant moral mediocrity, some comfortable but shoddy spiritual standard. This is a popular point of view. In fact, the psychologist Dr. Louis E. Bisch once urged people to "stop trying to be perfect."

This counsel has its appeal to the discouraged idealist. But it is not the counsel of Jesus Christ. The Christian is possessed of the spirit of Jesus. He faces only in one direction. He makes bonfires of all that stands in the way of his growth in godlikeness. He throws out the evil and burns up the cheap and undesirable. He cultivates the flowers and digs out the weeds. The superior life is not a matter of following rules. It is a matter of following God. And this means giving up the things that are against God. *Some things are wrong for the Christian not because they are evil, but because they keep him from being his best.* Our tolerance of the vulgar and the questionable does not make us happy; it only dilutes our Christian witness. Our righteousness must exceed the conformity of respectable people to the conventions of the day. We must avoid even the appearance of evil!

II

The Christian life demands *a superior sense of the goodness of God*. Henry Hitt Crane tells of a friend of his who began a promising career as a singer. This woman was endowed with great gifts of beauty and talent. She studied abroad with the finest teachers and was well on the way to becoming a star in concert and opera. Then she married a man who set out to quench her spirit and ambitions. Selfishly he subjected this singing spirit to insufferable domestic tyrannies. He imposed many petty restrictions and persecutions which succeeded in ruining her career. She endured all this with great patience. Finally her husband died, leaving her penniless. She supported herself and her growing daughter by giving music lessons. The hopes and promises of her younger days were now only a memory. She wrote a letter to Dr. Crane telling of her life and closing with these words, "Actually, I have done one thing down here on this earth: I have sung."

To this, Dr. Crane asked a natural question, "How could she sing? Thousands who have never had to endure a tithe of her suffering have grown silent, or their songs have soured into cynicism or self-pity; and yet she had kept singing—spiritually triumphant. How can one suffer so and never lose one's song?"

There is an answer to this question. It may be found in three lines by Victor Hugo:

> On a branch that swings
> Sits a bird that sings—
> Knowing that he has wings!

The Christian has the wings of the power of God! It is this that gives him the capacity to live triumphantly in the midst of in-

justice and evil and hate. The Christian character does not take
its color from its environment. The quality of its goodness is
supported by the resources of heaven. The Christian morality
does not return evil for evil. It sings its witness to the goodness
of God in the face of evil. The Christian returns good for bad.
The Christian loves when bitterness seems called for. No im-
moral acts of others can defeat the Christian. God has given him
wings. He knows that the eternal values which he represents
can never be destroyed. His righteousness exceeds the ordinary,
everyday righteousness of the crowd. It is this that makes him
superior in any society.

III

The Christian life demands *a superior sense of responsibility to
the duties that are clearly ours*. Most of us like to think we could
be knights in shining armor on some distant battlefield. We give
lip service to the larger issues of moral principle. But we are
woefully short in meeting the smaller issues squarely before us.

There is the woman, for instance, who wanted desperately to
get a start in newspaper work. She pictured herself as a famous
correspondent investigating and showing up the evil elements
of society. Then she saw herself as a famous photographer whose
pictures of the suffering people and unjust lot of millions of
mankind would help bring a better society into being. Her
imaginary exploits against the forces of darkness always brought
her world-wide influence and fame.

The tragedy was that there were plain, simple duties all around
her which she neglected in her daydreaming. Her husband
needed a sympathetic helpfulness which he did not get. Her aged
and infirm mother needed and yearned for her daughter's love
and care. The small community where she lived needed her
leadership in cleaning up evil conditions. A church nearby could
well have used her talents and help. Yet she felt no responsibility

31

at the very points where her goodness might have done some good. Because she could not do what she wanted, she refused to invest her life where it would have mattered.

This is the case with many Christians. We like to think of ourselves as members of the kingdom of God. But we do not deliver when it comes to making our Christian influence felt where we live. We believe in justice and morality and brotherhood in the abstract. But we do not recognize their claim on us in our own block. "Except your righteousness shall exceed." The Christian welcomes the responsibilities that are his. He gives himself to his nearby duties with a spirit that is shining and serene. He meets the challenge of his easily recognizable responsibilities. He is a Christian not only in society and before God, but to his own wife and children and within the circle of his most intimate friends. This is a mark of the superior life.

IV

The Christian life demands *a superior humility*. Jesus was suspicious of the righteousness of the Pharisees because they boasted about how good they were. They prided themselves on obeying all the rules and regulations. They admitted no faults. Their pride in their goodness diluted its value.

Pride in conventional morality is a common failing among Christians. We like to overrate ourselves, to pass for more than we are worth. This pride often gets us into trouble, as it did the young preacher who was called to the pulpit of a large New York church. He was quite proud of his attainment. His mother attended the installation service. The church was filled for the occasion. The atmosphere was solemn as the processional started up the long aisle. The young minister brought up the rear. He spotted his mother sitting at the end of a pew. As he passed her, he reached out and pinched her arm, whispering in her ear, "How'm I doing, Baby?" But as he went on, he noticed to his consternation that the woman was not his mother after all. She was one of his new parishioners!

Boastful vanity is foreign to Christian righteousness. Regardless of his moral attainments, the Christian remembers the spirit of Christ and is humbled before it. The egotistical spirit discounts Christian character. The true child of God is above all a genuine person. His goodness is real and solid and honest. He does not exhibit an inferiority complex by trying to pass for more than he is worth. The Christian is unassuming in his righteousness. It is a part of his very being and not something put on from the outside. As such it exceeds the ordinary righteousness. It is a mark of the superior life.

V

The Christian life demands *a superior human understanding*. The Pharisees liked to sit in judgment on their fellow man. They not only held themselves up as models of moral behavior, but they felt free to criticize those who broke the rules.

Far too many Christians today have the same idea. They confuse a legalistic morality for the Christian spirit. They find it easy to condemn, hard to forgive. They are quick to find fault, slow to understand. They like to judge but do not want to be judged. They are harsh in their attitudes toward others.

A man who lived close to a railroad yard was annoyed by the racket of the engines. To the officials of the road he wrote as follows: "Gentlemen: Why is it that your switch engine has to ding and dong and fizz and spit and bang and hiss and pant and grate and grind and puff and bump and chug and hoot and toot and whistle and wheeze and jar and jerk and howl and snarl and puff and growl and thump and boom and clash and jolt and screech and snort and slam and throb and roar and rattle and yell and smoke and smell and shriek all night long?"

In the same manner there are many people who irritate us no

end with their noisy personal frailties and foibles. We enjoy pointing our fingers in righteous indignation. To be sure, the Christian does not compromise moral principle; and many times we are guilty of too great a tolerance of moral illness. However, the righteousness of the Christian is no grim matter of puritanical repression. It is tempered by love and understanding and forgiveness. Jesus demonstrated many times that he regarded sins of the spirit more deadly than sins of the flesh. He found it easy to forgive penitent sinners but hard to deal with those who had obeyed the rules but whose hearts were hard and whose judgments were merciless. The strongest rebukes of the Master were directed toward the hypocrites and toward those who were prejudiced and harshly critical of their brothers. He told his followers to leave the judgment of man to God. A prim moral smugness is foreign to the sympathetic spirit of Jesus and often cancels out our Christian professions.

John Wesley's maxim has meaning for us at this point: "Do all the good you can, by all the means you can, in all the ways you can, in all the places you can, all the times you can, to all the people you can, as long as ever you can." Yes, and leave the rest with God. In other words, the emphasis of Christian righteousness is always positive, never negative. It is vital, active, living; superior to any code ever written.

VI

The Christian life demands *a superior sensitiveness to the moral laws of God*. The widespread breakdown of moral principle in high places is one of the tragic aspects of our time. To disregard old-fashioned honesty and integrity in everyday life is to undermine our boasted superiority as a Christian nation. To excuse public servants for wrongdoing on the flimsy excuse that "everybody is doing it" is to invite disaster. The goodness of the

Christian citizen must exceed the popular practices of the world.

This is not a concern only of the religious leader. It is a concern of all of us. A heartening indication of this concern is seen in the fact that an editorial on this subject in the St. Louis *Globe-Democrat* won the Pulitzer Prize for 1952. After reviewing the corruption and scandals of our day in government and out, the editorial closes with these words:

The time is here for moral regeneration. . . . The Roman Empire fell, not because it was overwhelmed from without, but because it decayed from within. If this is an appeal for a return to the day-by-day practice of old-time religion, and respect for God's moral law, so be it. When the moral fabric of a nation begins to unravel, it is time to do some patching before the entire garment is gone.

Here is the clue for our recovery. For men of unimpeachable honor are, first of all, men of God. It is a sense of God that alone can put into life the moral stamina that makes men and nations superior in quality and power.

CHAPTER FOUR

*"Ye have heard that it was said by them of old time,'
Thou shalt not kill; and whosoever shall kill shall be
in danger of the judgment: but I say unto you, That
whosoever is angry with his brother without a cause
shall be in danger of the judgment: and whosoever
shall say to his brother, Raca shall be in danger of the
council: but whosoever shall say, Thou fool, shall be in
danger of hell fire. Therefore if thou bring thy gift to
the altar, and there rememberest that thy brother hath
ought against thee; leave there thy gift before the
altar, and go thy way; first be reconciled to thy
brother, and then come and offer thy gift. Agree with
thine adversary quickly, whiles thou art in the way
with him; lest at any time the adversary deliver thee
to the judge, and the judge deliver thee to the officer,
and thou be cast into prison. Verily I say unto thee,
Thou shalt by no means come out thence, till thou hast
paid the uttermost farthing."* —Matthew 5:21-26

THE BROTHERLY LIFE

Therefore if thou bring thy gift to the altar, and
there rememberest that thy brother hath ought
against thee; leave there thy gift before the altar,
and go thy way; first be reconciled to thy brother,
and then come and offer thy gift.

ONE of Tolstoi's lesser known works is his
play called *Light Shining in Darkness*. It
is the story of Nicolai Ivanovitsch
Sarynzev. This man makes an effort to live by the Sermon on
the Mount. He rids himself of his property. He attempts to earn
his living as a joiner. He causes his daughter's fiancé to revolt

against army service. He brings unhappiness to his family. He finds in the end that as far as he is concerned, the Sermon on the Mount is not practical in our world. He has tried to take it literally, even radically, and it has not worked for him. At least not according to his interpretation of it.

Many would agree with Nicolai Ivanovitsch Sarynzev. The message of the Master often seems beyond us. There are many others, however, who try also to follow its divine guidance and who find in it a light shining in darkness. These would agree with such a one, E. Stanley Jones, when he said, "The Sermon on the Mount is the transcript of Jesus' mind and spirit. It commands our reverence and respect, but more—it commands our obedience and our very all. It is a working philosophy of life— the only one that will work, for the universe backs this way of life."

There is no teaching of the Sermon that is more difficult and yet has so many possibilities as the emphasis of Jesus on the treatment of our brother men. "Love your enemies." "Bless them that curse you." "Do not resist one who is evil" (R.S.V.) These are spiritual mountain peaks that both lure us and baffle us. Who is sufficient for these things? Yet who would want to remove them? We are humbled and challenged because they are there. We can at least set our faces in their direction. It is important to have the ideal even though we may never completely attain it.

Jesus takes up the subject of the brotherly life in a strong statement against anger and hatred. He declares that the judgment of God will be against those who are angry with their brothers and who call their brother men fools. He points up the idea of reconciliation as one of the keys to true brotherhood.

I

Jesus is saying *the Christian takes the initiative in reconciliation as a means of breaking down barriers of enmity*. The Bible sometimes speaks of reconciliation of man with God. Jesus is here, however, speaking of reconciliation with our fellow men. If anger or hatred has come between men, the Christian is not to rest until he has made amends. The dictionary definition of reconciliation is, "Restoration to friendship." The point is, therefore, that broken human relations can be repaired by the magic of Christian forgiveness, patience, and understanding. *But the effort must be made!* Reconciliation will not come with wishful thinking, or even through prayer. In fact, says Jesus, we are to leave so important a thing as our own worship and go make our peace with our brothers from whom we have been estranged. This is as hard a thing as any of us will ever be called on to do. We shrink from it. Yet it is urgent and pressing business.

Henry Sloane Coffin tells an interesting incident which occurred when he was a pastor. There were two women in his congregation who were at daggers' points with each other. They were leading members of the church. Formerly good friends, they now positively refused to speak or associate in any way. This deep rift was hurting them and hurting the church. Dr. Coffin decided the time had come to take a hand. One day he checked to be sure one of them was at home. Then he took the other in his car on a church errand. He stopped at the home of the first. When she opened the door, the two women stood facing each other in consternation. Neither spoke nor moved. Then the preacher pushed his companion inside and quickly closed the door from the outside. He stayed without for half an hour and then opened the door cautiously. The two women were laughing and weeping at the same time in each other's arms. They remained fast friends for life.

The sooner we take this initiative in asking forgiveness or in righting wrongs, the better and easier it is. Resentments and grudges have a way of becoming fixed with time. Then they fester and are hard to heal. So many times we become angry and hateful without actually knowing the other side of the story. It takes a person with a big heart and strong courage to admit to another that he has wronged him.

The famous Scottish professor John Stuart Blackie required his students to hold their book in the left hand when they stood up to recite. One day a new student stood up with his book in his right hand. Professor Blackie protested. "The other hand, please!" But the student read on, ignoring the request.

Again Blackie spoke with anger, "Do you hear me? The left hand!" There was a moment of silence. Then the student held up a stump of a left arm. It was all he had! Then John Stuart Blackie, great spirit that he was, rushed from his place and knelt down at the student's feet and cried, "Can you ever forgive me, sir?" You see, we easily find fault often without knowing the facts involved.

"Go . . . ; first be reconciled to thy brother." This principle of the necessity of initiative in reconciliation is a very real and practical thing. We tend to slur it over because it is strong medicine. This is one reason our religion is so unreal to us and our personal relations become so tangled. We don't want to forgive, and we don't want to ask forgiveness. But few experiences can contribute so much to our happiness. Members of Alcoholics Anonymous have discovered this. One of their basic requirements in a man's fight against alcoholism is this very point. A person must set down for himself every wrong he has done another as an alcoholic. The lies, the broken engagements, the unpaid bills. He must make amends to every person he has harmed! This is a tough assignment. But the result is freedom and joy and self-mastery.

A very wise man suggested one time that we have a "Day of Forgiveness" as a time of general reconciliation. He said: "Suppose we think of every ornery creature who's ever stabbed us, slapped us, kicked us in the shins, or hit us in the solar plexus, cheated us or cursed us, ignored, snubbed or slighted us. Then on this holy day suppose we get them all together in the tank of our memory, and turn the hose on them until we drown them in the waters of forgiveness." It's a good idea! Not only for individuals, but for a church. But the Christian dare not wait for such a special observance on the part of everyone else. He sets for himself his own Day of Reconciliation. He will find it a glorious occasion.

II

Jesus is saying *Christian reconciliation is a prerequisite to fellowship with God.* As has been suggested, we talk a great deal in Christian circles about getting right with God. But, according to Jesus, getting right with man is more important still. In our text Jesus is saying that no one can be in tune with God who is not on speaking terms with his neighbor. The Master repeats this idea later in the Sermon in the two verses that immediately follow the Lord's Prayer. "For if ye forgive men their trespasses, your heavenly Father will also forgive you: but if ye forgive not men their trespasses, neither will your Father forgive your trespasses." This is plain speaking!

The point is that our relationship with God is an inward, spiritual thing. We may go through the outward form of worship even with hearts that bear ill will toward our brother men. But it does us no good. For God looks upon the hearts and motives of men. And when our spirits are bitter with resentments and grudges toward others, our attempted adoration of God is an empty effort. "First be reconciled to thy brother, and then come and offer thy gift."

The transcription of a religious radio program comes to mind. The beautiful music spoke of love and understanding among men. The speaker's message was a pointed discussion of Christian brotherhood. But the label on the jacket of the record read like this: "Fingerprints will be reproduced as audible disturbances on this transcription. Please avoid fingerprinting the grooves by handling the record by the outside rim." This is a parable of life and worship. For the voice of God and the heavenly harmonies may be distorted and marred by minor human disturbances. Petty prejudices, little misunderstandings, selfish unconcern for the rights of others, harsh words, may seem little enough to us. But such are the fingerprints of irritation which all too often block our hearts from the ministry of the divine. And too often they also block the spirit of Christ in the fellowship of the church.

This section of the Sermon on the Mount begins with these words: "Ye have heard that it was said by them of old time, Thou shalt not kill; and whosoever shall kill shall be in danger of the judgment: but I say unto you, That whosoever is angry with his brother without a cause shall be in danger of the judgment." Therefore, in this case, as in the later teachings about adultery and retaliation, Jesus is declaring a new law. He is saying that outer conformity to the old law against killing is not enough. He declares that we are to be judged rather by the inner desires of our hearts. Outward conformity to rules alone is not sufficient for God. Our inner attitudes of hate and anger are enough to estrange ourselves from him. This is a tremendous step forward in moral and religious teaching. It lies at the very heart of the Christian gospel.

Under the older law God could be placated by one's bringing gifts to the Temple. These might be bulls and cows or doves or incense or even offerings of money. These sacrifices and offerings are useless, said Jesus, unless the mind and heart are free from offense. The offense need not be the anger that might lead to murder. The Master said that if you are trying to pray and "rememberest that thy brother hath *ought* against thee"—thus even our feelings of spite and undue pride of superiority may keep us from the throne of heaven. The desire to punish other people or see them punished can do the same. Likewise, the wish to "get even" and the attitude that "it serves him right" are things that form a barrier to spiritual power and maturity. *Many earnest Christians who are particular about their religious beliefs and habits need to exhibit a more charitable and understanding spirit toward their fellow men.*

Therefore, our inmost thoughts must be offered on the altar of God if we are to know him as he is. We must come clean with God and man. This is spiritual discipline of the highest order. Not many of us can live up to it. But only as we try, can we hope to grow in the knowledge and love of God. This discipline searches our souls to their depths. It also offers a way to spiritual victory and personal integrity. A great many self-righteous and pious people must learn to exercise this discipline.

III

Jesus is also saying here that *the spirit of reconciliation is a necessary part of a healthy personality.* In this contrast between the old law and the new, Jesus is saying that anger itself (he is not speaking here of righteous indignation) is as deadly as murder. Contempt and sneers can kill other people's spirits. But most of all, hate and enmity can fasten themselves on us with a fierce and death-dealing grip. These are destructive emotions. They tear us apart. They warp our judgment. They break down our personal poise and peace of mind. They bring on high blood pressure and nervous disorders. They fasten themselves on our vital organs and cause organic illness and death. These facts are confirmed by leading physicians and medical clinics. It is, therefore, no arbitrary ruling when Jesus says that we must get right with our brothers before we try to worship God. True worship requires whole and dedicated personalities. These are impossible so long as the spirit is sick with the germs of prejudice, suspicion, rancor,. and resentment. We owe it to our own personal well-being to rid ourselves of them. We must do so if we are to enjoy true fellowship with the heavenly Father.

This teaching of Jesus thus has a very practical and health-giving value. It touches us all in some degree. In fact, one expert personal counselor reported that he found more people upset physically and spiritually by resentments and hates than by sex problems. Sometimes these influences are subconscious. But they are none the less deadly. We would all be healthier and happier personalities if we would surrender our feelings of ill will in the spirit of Christian forgiveness and reconciliation.

There are those modern, materialistic-minded sophisticates who would question all this. They say that what is done is done and nothing can alter it. Yet the forgiving and healing powers of God are demonstrated in the simplest forms of nature. N. Bishop Harman, Fellow of the Royal College of Surgeons of England, in his book *Science and Religion* tells at some length of the strange powers and efforts of nature to restore things to their former state after an offense has been committed.

Dr. Harman points to the healing of a wound in the tissues of the body. There is an immediate and united effort of the bodily structure for the repair of the injury. The fluids of the body exude in an attempt to close the wound. The wandering cells of the body collect about the wound to ward off an alien invasion. Then the fixed tissue cells erect a scaffolding over the break. The process of repair goes on until nothing is left but a clean white seam in place of a gaping, bleeding wound. This surgeon declares that there is more wonder and precision in this healing process than there is in the construction of a great building. The same process likewise takes place in more delicate lesions of the nerves and brain cells.

There are other examples. There is the pine tree. When the tree is but a sapling, the leading shoot may be torn off. The wound is repaired, and another shoot is put forth, which grows upright into a straight, tall tree. Even the scars of earth are healed over. The injuries of war are forgiven by nature. In time the ugly trenches will be gone. The barbed wire will rust into dust. Wind and rain and sun and flowers cover over what has been.

Therefore, says Dr. Harman: "Is it less so with man, who is also a part of nature? . . . Forgiveness is almost a part of our life." Indeed, it must be a part if we are to live in happiness and at peace with ourselves and our neighbors. Why should we curse the wrongs done to us and the ill will borne us, and thus stupidly hold out against the universal pattern of healing that God has built into the universe itself?

Yet this is what we so often try to do. And it never works. Here is the case of a woman who lived in resentment for many long, unhappy years. In her girlhood she had been wronged by a man. A fierce hatred set in. "For two years," she said, "I shut myself up in my room and did not speak to anyone during that time. I nursed my hate." Later a psychoanalyst told her she must not continue to hate, or she would set up a complex. She came to a wise minister of souls for help. She said, "I have hated all these years, but it has worn me out. I'm sick of this hating. It is killing me." The minister told her that by the grace of God she must change her attitude to one of positive love toward this man. She reluctantly did so. She wrote him and offered to help him. In doing this simple thing she released herself from the grip of this nightmare that had been sapping her life. She became a radiant and useful person from that moment on.

"Therefore if thou bring thy gift to the altar, and there re-memberest that thy brother hath ought against thee; leave there thy gift before the altar, and go thy way; first be reconciled to thy brother, and then come and offer thy gift." This is the door of a new life for us.

CHAPTER FIVE

> *"It hath been said, Whosoever shall put away his wife, let him give her a writing of divorcement: but I say unto you, That whosoever shall put away his wife, saving for the cause of fornication, causeth her to commit adultery: and whosoever shall marry her that is divorced committeth adultery."*
>
> —Matthew 5:31-32

THE LOYAL LIFE

> But I say unto you, That whosoever shall put away his wife, saving for the cause of fornication, causeth her to commit adultery.

DEAN Inge, in *A Rustic Moralist*, told of the experience of a New York physician. This doctor asked a hundred married men and a hundred married women this question: "If by some miracle you could press a button and find that you had never been married to your husband or wife, would you press the button?" One hundred and thirty out of the two hundred said, "No." Sixteen said, "No," with qualifications. And only twenty-eight said, "Yes."

These results are encouraging. It is good to know that there are many couples living together who have not regretted the adventure of marriage to the point of wanting to wipe out the experience. The trouble is, however, that there is no magic button conveniently handy when the strains and tensions of marriage appear. Where the divorce court is considered undesirable, this often means that a state of armed truce exists. It is not the actual breakup of marriages that is the most important problem before most married couples. It is the problem of getting marriage off dead level and making it the happy and exciting reality of their dreams. Few couples want divorce. Most couples do not expect Utopia. But all couples have a right to find in marriage a rich and satisfying program of living.

Jesus' words on divorce are plain. We must not minimize or evade them. However, the Master was no legalist. He was concerned always with the highest interests of men and women. He wanted them to make marriage a blessed and enduring relationship. Only so could it mean the most to their well-being. To this end he sharply emphasized the desirability of permanence in marriage. This calls for loyalties of a high order. Could this be the real objective of Jesus' teaching at this point?

Marriage does not have to be perfect to be happy and creative and permanent. There is a vast middle ground where many couples live and where most of the troubles in marriage arise. For instance, take the case of the Marburys. Things weren't serious. They just weren't getting along as well as they should. Analysis showed that the husband was making some mistakes. He was dogmatic and pompous and ignored his wife's opinions. He dressed sloppily at home and neglected personal manners. He was unsympathetic to his wife's health and thought her illness an excuse to avoid housework. He refused to take her out socially. But, on the other hand, these were the wife's mistakes: she disliked housekeeping and neglected her home; she was extravagant with family funds; she resented the role of housewife and preferred a career; she enjoyed innocent flirtations and competed for other men's attention.

As is usually the case, both parties were to blame. As is frequently the case, the Marburys needed to give serious attention to the fundamentals of happiness in marriage. As is often the case, a new sense of personal loyalty growing out of a renewed religious faith helped them to put their marriage on a sound footing and on a higher plane of personal happiness. This can usually be the case if *both parties* are willing to work at the job.

What are some of the loyalty factors that lift marriage above the ordinary and make it the blessed institution it should be?

I

The ideal of marriage must be high, realistic, and mutually agreed upon. Dr. Randolph Ray, rector of the famous "Little Church Around the Corner" in New York, said that the cure for easy divorce is hard marriage. This would likely be Jesus' solution also. Dr. Ray refuses to marry more couples than he marries. Many times, in the course of conversation with the prospective bride and groom he finds that one of them will say that if this marriage does not prove to be successful, they can always get a divorce. When this view is expressed before the ceremony, Dr. Ray says it puts the marriage under a handicap which is impossible to overcome. Divorce comes easily when marriage is regarded lightly. Like the Texarkana, Texas, husband who sued his fifteen-year-old wife for divorce on the grounds that "she acted like a child"! Or like the Lansing, Michigan, man, wed only four weeks, who asked for a divorce on the grounds that his eyeglasses were out of focus when he married!

In other words, permanence in marriage is often predetermined by the attitude of both parties toward marriage itself. If one of them regards marriage as a matter of convenience, or as a means of getting along in the world, or of licensed sexual gratification, or as a way out of a problem situation, such a marriage is doomed before it starts. Likewise, marriage is no magical route to happiness for two people of widely differing educational background, cultural interests, religious training, and philosophies of life.

One of the most important studies of marriage has been made by the psychologist Lewis H. Terman and other psychologists at Stanford University. The results are in his book *Psychological Factors in Marital Happiness*. The studies show that of all the influences that determine a happy marriage, the four most important are: 1. Having parents who are happily married and who set their children a good example of how a happy marriage works. 2. Having a mature character and effective personality. All the habits contributing to character and personality contribute also to a happy marriage. 3. Being religious and being married under the auspices of a church. 4. Being eager to have children or to adopt children. By inference, the factors of romantic love or physical passion are of far less importance than we usually think.

The point is, marriage is a serious business and can affect human life for good or ill more than any one other personal program. Yet most people enter into it with little or no preparation. We prepare our young people for careers of all kinds. Yet we trust to luck in the most important career of all, the career of wife or husband.

A hundred years ago today a wilderness was here;
A man with powder in his gun went forth to hunt a deer.
But now the times have changed somewhat along a different plan;
A dear with powder on her nose goes forth to hunt a man!

With the desire "to get a man" the controlling factor in so many lives, it is little wonder so many marriages turn out unhappily, if not disastrously.

Will Durant, historian and philosopher, has given us these ten commandments for modern youth: 1. I will never do to others what I would not have done to me. 2. I will keep my body healthy and my mind clear by temperance in everything. 3. I will prepare myself in youth to be a good mate and a provident parent. 4. I will choose a mate not for beauty or wealth, but for character, health, and intelligence. 5. I will enter marriage

with a mind to make it a sacred union lasting through all difficulties, until death. 6. I will have children, and will rear them in
loving discipline. 7. I will never cheat or bribe, or accept a bribe
in any form. 8. I will never exploit my fellow man. 9. I will
repay my community and my country for the protection and
opportunities it offers me. 10. I will continue my education in
health, character, and intelligence until my death.[1]

When two young people, both of whom have lived by such
a code, come together in marriage, the marriage may reasonably
be expected to be well above the average in permanence and in
happiness. This is because such lives are loyal lives. They are
loyal to the best values, loyal to themselves, loyal to others, and
loyal to God. Divorce is beyond the thinking of such couples.

This ideal of marriage must be close to the thinking of the
Master. In his characteristic dramatic way, he faced his listeners
with the necessity of regarding marriage as an experience both
blessed and lasting.

II

*The practical problems of marriage can be solved with good
humor and common sense on both sides.* David Randall, head
of the rare-book department of Scribner's, tells the story of the
sale of an interesting document. It was General Robert E. Lee's
famous General Order No. 9, issued to his commanders in the
field when Lee surrendered at Appomattox. Mr. Randall offered
this on page 54 of Catalogue No. 137. As soon as the catalogue
was out, a long-distance call came from someone who wanted
to buy the item for the stated price of $450. Mr. Randall asked
the buyer why he wanted it, since he was not a collector. The
purchaser said, "Occasionally I get into disagreements with my
wife and children. I want to frame Lee's message and hang it

[1] From Executives' Club *News*, Oct. 5, 1951. Used by permission.

above my desk to remind me how to accept defeat gracefully."

Lee's General Order No. 9 begins: "After four years of arduous service marked by unsurpassed courage and fortitude, the Army of Northern Virginia has been compelled to yield to overwhelming numbers and resources."

This spirit of good-humored give and take is necessary for a happy marriage. Trouble comes when one party always wants to take everything and never wants to give. Husbands and wives both need to be reminded that retreat and surrender are often the better part of valor. It takes more than stubborn pride, "arduous service," and "unsurpassed courage" to make a marriage work successfully. We make progress as we learn how to co-operate, how to overlook little annoyances, and how to accept defeat gracefully.

A man in Detroit choked his wife to death with a towel. They had been childhood sweethearts and had been married twenty-nine years. "She was a jewel when I married her," he said, "but she got lazy. She wore a hole in the living-room rug sitting in one place to work jigsaw puzzles while my underwear went unmended." In the meantime, however, his wife had been working in an office and had taken in two roomers to augment his small income. That couple, like all couples, had their problems. Far better, however, for the wife to mend underwear than be choked to death! Far better for the husband to wear underwear with holes than to be tried for murder! Lives that are basically loyal can forgive, endure, and overcome.

The point is that most practical problems of marriage can be solved if both parties want to solve them. In fact, the problems themselves can help build a stronger marriage if they are attacked together with intelligence and a sense of humor. Someone has listed these rules on how to make quarrels improve your marriage: 1. Realize that some conflict between married people is inevitable. 2. Don't try to reform your mate. 3. Don't bury your grievances. 4. Stick to the issues while quarreling. Don't go off on tangents of personal abuse. 5. Don't worry about who's right or wrong. Be quick to apologize, even though you are right. 6. Grant your mate the right to be difficult once in a while. 7. Be patient but not long-suffering. 8. Try to end the quarrel on a constructive note. Agree on steps to solve the problem. 9. If quarrels become chronic, don't wait until your marriage is ruined. Consult some expert outsider.

In other words, if there is a serious point at issue, such as relatives or finances, attack it and settle it and forget it. It is the running, long-term, never-ending nagging and complaining and criticizing and whining that cast a dark blot over marriage. Come to terms with the big problems and overlook the little ones. That way lies happiness in marriage. A sense of devout loyalty can do this for us. Marriage needs more self-discipline and less self-indulgence. Here is the sharp thrust of Jesus' teaching.

III

The little niceties of good human relations must never be forgotten. A Kafir tribe in Africa has an odd wedding custom. The wedding ceremony takes all day. Sometime during the day the bride will rise up and break into a fury of temper against the man she is marrying. She screams in great rage and denounces the groom with every vile word she can think of. He is a mass of rottenness, she shouts. He is the ugliest man she has ever seen. He is mean and selfish. His mother should have choked him when he was a boy. It makes her sick to look at him, she says. She wonders why any sensible girl would ever marry such a lump of stupidity.

This outburst is all quite in order. It is the custom of the tribe. After the marriage the wife is not supposed to talk back or act mean to her husband. Therefore she is given a chance to get it all out of her system before the marriage begins!

This practice may seem a bit uncivilized. But the principle is civilized. Too often we put on our best manners before marriage and our worst manners after the ceremony is over. This is enough to make any marriage unworkable. Why should we persist in unloading our worst attitudes within the sacred confines of the home? Marriage deserves our gentlest spirit, our kindest words, our finest personal relationships. To use the marriage state as an excuse to vent our meanness, our irritations, our selfish whims, is to betray its meaning and destroy its possibilities. Husbands and wives both had better get rid of their ugly tempers and carping criticisms before the wedding ceremony occurs. Afterward we should hold our peace. Mean dispositions spoil many more marriages than infidelity. They should be stopped beforehand, for they will surely wreck a marriage afterward. The wedding ceremony has no magic whereby a boor becomes a gentleman or a shrew a saint.

Marriages thrive on small attentions and generous considerations. Politeness, courtesy, and understanding on both sides will do more for a marriage than a big income or a fine house. Frequent compliments and appreciation will overcome many a limitation in culture or ability. Plain thoughtfulness and simple tenderness mean more than extravagant promises. The spirit of mature understanding and forgiveness will last far longer than social glamour and sexual thrills. Our marriages are in our own hands. We can make them or break them by the kind of people we ourselves choose to be. When we loyally hold ourselves up to our highest loyalties, we bring the other person up also.

I love you not only for what you are, but for what I am when I am with you. I love you not only for what you have made of yourself, but for what you are making of me. I love you for passing over all the foolish, weak things that you can't help dimly seeing in my heart, and for drawing out into the light all the beautiful belongings that no one else had looked quite far enough to find. I love you because you are helping me to make of the lumber of my life, not a tavern but a temple and out of the works of my every day, not a reproach but a song. I love you because you have done more than any creed could have done to make me happy. You have done it without a touch, without a word, without a sign. You have done it by just being yourself.

Yes, a love that makes us better people never fails to cement lives together and make for happiness.

IV

The atmosphere of married life must be sanctified and purified by a vital religious faith. If marriage is to last, its loyalties must be based on something more than mere physical, material, and social arrangements. Monogamous marriage is a sacred and spiritual union sanctioned by God and blessed by Jesus Christ. It works best and gives the highest satisfactions when it is based on the laws of God and conducted in the spirit of the Master. This fact is written into the records of marriage clinics and divorce courts. They show that couples married in a religious ceremony have a much lower rate of divorce than do couples married in a civil ceremony. Persons who have been brought up in the church and Sunday school make much better marriage partners than those who have not. Couples who attend church together regularly from the beginning of their married life are much more likely to be happy and adjusted than those who do not. Nothing binds hearts closer together than a deep and real faith in God. When couples pray together and sing hymns together and serve together, they are likely to be able to meet any of the issues of life with triumphant power and sacrificial love. The germs of so-called incompatibility have little chance to grow and multiply in the cleansing sunlight of God's presence. A common loyalty to God makes the loyalties of marriage sacred and secure. When God joins together a couple, it is almost impossible for man to break it asunder.

The English preacher Alistair Maclean said that we must think of ourselves as commissioned by God in every role of life. "I am a God-appointed farmer. I am a God-appointed wife, I am a God-appointed laborer, I am a God-appointed nurse. Therefore I occupy a place of sacred trust, and to it I must offer my loving loyalty—a loyalty as sure as the sunrising; as constant as the tide, and as glad and generous as a woman's self-giving to her child." A God-appointed wife! A God-appointed husband! Here is that which gives urgency and glamour and beauty and adventure to the building of a home. It is this divine undergirding that gives refinement and nobility to married life.

Dean Randolph Ray, after twenty years of advising and marrying fifty thousand couples, gives these five simple rules for happiness in marriage: 1. Be kind. 2. Remember marriage is a partnership. 3. Don't lose your temper. 4. Don't postpone making up after a quarrel. 5. Cultivate faith in God and faith in each other. Such marriages are both permanent and blessed. They are a living expression of the loyalty that is basic to Jesus' idea of marriage. His teaching against divorce will become a reality in our modern world when we are willing to concentrate on making marriage an enduring relationship based on Christian principles.

CHAPTER SIX

"Ye have heard that it hath been said, An eye for an eye, and a tooth for a tooth: but I say unto you, That ye resist not evil: but whosoever shall smite thee on thy right cheek, turn to him the other also. And if any man will sue thee at the law, and take away thy coat, let him have thy cloke also. And whosoever shall compel thee to go a mile, go with him twain. Give to him that asketh thee, and from him that would borrow of thee turn not thou away."   *—Matthew 5:38-42*

THE WILLING LIFE

Whosoever shall compel thee to go a mile,
go with him twain.

SOME time ago a display of modern art was held at the Metropolitan Museum of Art in New York City. American sculptors, painters, and other artists competed for a total of $52,000 in awards. The first-place award went to an Illinois artist. The picture was not a pleasant one. It merely showed a closed door bearing a funeral wreath. Underneath was the title, "That which I should have done, I did not do." This is a grim reminder of the minimum kind of living most of us engage in. Most of us do just as little as we can. We are ruled by the routine. We go so far and no farther. We live to ourselves and for ourselves. We answer no high challenge. We hedge and draw back and are afraid to go beyond the custom of the crowd. We drudgingly fulfill the necessary obligations of life, but we don't like to do more than is required.

The statement of the second-mile principle is part of a series of similar statements by Jesus. They are expressions of the new law of inner loyalty to an ideal rather than conformity to an older law of retaliation or revenge. "Ye have heard that it hath been said, An eye for an eye, and a tooth for a tooth: but I say unto you, That ye resist not evil: but whosoever shall smite thee on the right cheek, turn to him the other also. And if any man will sue thee at the law, and take away thy coat, let him have thy cloke also. And whosoever shall compel thee to go a mile, go with him twain."

Thus did Jesus challenge the principle that the wrongdoer should get as good as he gave, as was required by the Mosaic law, the Code of Hammurabi, and the Roman law. The Master wanted to release men from the terrible burden of this law of the jungle. He was telling them that the new idea was the strategy of victory over their oppressors. He knew that the vengeful spirit reacts against us in the long run and holds us slaves. This is true of all the oppressions of life, of which there are many. Here is an amazing idea—we win over our enemies and over our obstacles not by resisting them, but by going them one better! Nothing can more quickly deflate our antagonists!

In this business of the second mile, Jesus seems to be trying to tell us, therefore, that rebellious living is all wrong. It can lead only to closed doors, vain regrets, and barren lives. The positive, sympathetic, generous spirit gets results even in difficult situations.

In other words, Jesus is holding before us the secret of the power of willingness, which is one of the most releasing and dynamic forces in life. It is this power of willingness that often is the difference between failure and success, defeat and victory, surrender and triumph. The power of willingness is the difference between dull existence and adventurous living. It is the difference between a prosaic and harmless Christianity on the one hand and a vital, joyous experience of faith on the other. Indeed, the program of the kingdom of God waits on willing, eager workers.

This principle of the power of willingness operates for great living in every department of life—personal happiness, careers, home, and church. It has everyday applications in addition to its original meaning.

I

The power of willingness *overcomes weaknesses and magnifies small talents.* A man by the name of Bruno Furst is said to have the most remarkably memory in the world. After reading a copy of the Sunday *New York Times*, he can describe in detail what is on each of the seventy pages in any order. He knows by memory most of Schiller's plays, all of Goethe's *Faust*, much of Heine and Thomas Mann, scores of novels and plays. In his mind he has stored the population and area of every American city of over 100,000 population, to say nothing of the names of the most important way stations on every major railroad in the world. He knows most of the important dates of recorded history and the day of the week on which they fell. Mention any two places on the earth's surface, and he'll supply the geography in between: mountains with heights, rivers with lengths, lakes with depths, cities with populations, and countries with areas.

The point is, he is no genius. Far from it. In fact, at the age of ten, Bruno Furst was the class dunce. He could not remember the alphabet. He bogged down in school on the two-by-two table. He went completely to pieces on the rivers of Germany. In college he took up the study of law, but he realized he had no memory. In the University of Munich, at the time, was a famous specialist in memory training, Dr. Poehlmann. Bruno decided to study to develop his memory. Dr. Poehlmann told him that the memory, like a muscle, can be trained to grow and develop. Bruno Furst willingly exercised, trained, and constantly practiced his memory. Month after month he gave himself to this objective. When he graduated from law school, the onetime school dunce could repeat verbatim the entire German Civil Code, some 2,385 paragraphs of legal verbiage filling five thick volumes. What's the point of all this? The *power of willingness* took a notably bad memory and made it amazingly effective!

Some years ago a little boy by the name of Angelo Siciliano was born the son of Italian immigrants in Brooklyn. He lived in the slums and was a scrawny, thin, undernourished lad. In fact, at sixteen he weighed only ninety-seven pounds and was a pale, nervous runt, an easy prey for bullies. One day in the lobby of the Brooklyn Museum, where he had gone with boys from the Italian Settlement House, he became entranced with the statues of the Greek gods, especially Hercules. He could hardly believe that these statues had been posed by men. He had never known that men could have such perfect and powerful bodies. He decided that he would make himself over into the likeness of a Greek god. He started by clipping a series of exercises from a newspaper. He had no fancy gymnasium equipment. This did not stop him, for he devised his own system of tensing his muscles and playing one against another.

It was hard work. The other boys made fun of him. His enemies sneered at his feeble display of muscles. But he was determined to reach his goal. Year after year he willingly slaved away at his exercises. To make a long story short, the skinny runt from Brooklyn became known as Charles Atlas, the world's most perfectly developed man. He, too, had the body of a god. For it was said of him that he possessed the "true classic physique, in perfect proportions, a blend of Hercules and Apollo." Not only that, but like the Greeks who modeled for the statues of the immortals, Charles Atlas has posed for the statues of the great.

Among these are the ones of Alexander Hamilton in front of the Treasury Building in Washington and George Washington on the Washington Square monument in New York. Again, it was a triumph of the *power of willingness!*

The point is simple but important. Everyone has certain basic capacities in life. However limited they may be, they can always be increased by willing effort. God has provided for the expansion of our talents. Thank God man can grow! He grows as he is willing to try. No one compelled Bruno Furst and Angelo Siciliano to do what they did. They were propelled from within. God blesses those who are willing to start. This is why the power of willingness is often a greater asset than superior talent. Our very deficiencies become our assets when we are claimed by some inward drive.

This, Jesus is saying, is the genius of the Christian idea in the realm of the spirit. God does not compel men to be good. Our minds are attracted by the mind of God. Our souls are lured by the hope of becoming like gods. It is then that we ourselves give ourselves without being driven. When we do this, we discover within ourselves undreamed-of capacities for great Christian living. Let no one belittle his own abilities. The power of willingness can reveal the true stuff of which we are made. God cannot use large talents if they remain hidden and indifferent. But God can take small talents, if they are willingly dedicated, and make them grow and multiply.

II

The power of willingness *takes the drudgery out of hard tasks.* Harry Emerson Fosdick told about the time his mother sent him to pick a quart of raspberries, when he was a boy. He did not want to pick a quart of raspberries. He dragged himself in a rebellious mood to the berry patch. He was resentful of a world in which little boys had to pick raspberries when they wanted to do something else. Then he had an idea. It might be fun to pick two quarts of raspberries instead of one and surprise the family. He said, "I had so interesting a time picking two quarts of raspberries, to the utter amazement of the household, that, although it happened nearly half a century ago, I have never forgotten it. . . . What the circumstances and compulsions of life do to us depends upon what they find in us."

Life makes demands on us to go and to do. The first mile under the requirements of duty is no stranger to any of us. There are some things we have to do. There are other things we are made to do. But if we do no more than these things, we become wretched victims of human slavery. Jesus tells us how we can escape such unhappy bondage. It is not by resistance or rebellion. It is rather by the simple process of doing more than is expected of us! The sting of the first-mile drudgery is relieved as we willingly go on to the second mile. Even the hardest jobs become a joy when we find it is more fun to willingly pick two quarts of raspberries than to pick one quart under pressure.

This idea has meaning in every area of life. It has meaning for the disciplines of the spirit and the tasks of the kingdom of God. We resist the call of God because we are apt to think of the Christian life as a matter of requirements and demands. From one aspect the Christian life appears to consist of distasteful duties. This is a complete misreading of the entire idea. For the disciplines of the Christian faith come from within. As Christians we don't give up some things and do other things because we have to, but because we want to. And this makes all the difference in the world. It makes all the difference, too, in getting done the difficult jobs of a more Christian society.

A young American plastic surgeon, Dr. Ralph Blocksma, served in England during World War II. He was stationed at Wheatly, just outside Oxford. Here he was able to restore the shattered bodies and faces of many of the boys who were casualties of the Normandy landing. After a boy who was one of the worst of these casualties had been made to appear as good as new, the chaplain of the outfit congratulated the doctor. He said, "Ralph, you have miracles in your fingers! Miracles in your fingers because God has put miracles in your heart!"

After the war Dr. Blocksma returned to Chicago, and his career developed rapidly. The future was bright. Then he wrote a letter to the chaplain who had been with him at the Ninety-seventh General Hospital in England during the war. In it he said in part:

I'm on the threshold of what could become quite a lucrative career in plastic surgery. But here is the payoff. It isn't what I want. Ruth and I and the kids are sailing as medical missionaries for Lahore, Pakistan. It was a long, difficult, and sometimes soul-crushing road that led me to abandon my own selfish ambitions for a total surrender to Christ—but, oh brother, what fun it is! This is powerful stuff. This is dynamite. I thought I was sacrificing, but every time I consciously tried, I got back ten times more than I had given. . . . So many have wondered what can move a man in my position to shove off for a heathen land. I never could say it before, but now, "For me to live is Christ"—and from dawn to dark, I love it! [1]

Well, that's the way it works! From picking raspberries to remaking the face of the world, the tough jobs of life lose their terror to those who are captured by this strange power of willingness. Jesus knew it to be so.

III

The power of willingness *guarantees results*. Years ago two seniors in a certain university were competing for school honors in grades. One night, as one of the boys was turning off his light

---

[1] Grant S. King, "Miracles in His Fingers," in *Christian Herald*. Used by permission of the author and *Christian Herald*.

to go to bed, he noticed the light of his competitor still burning. The next night he stayed up until the other light went out and then kept on studying for one hour longer. He repeated the same thing each night. When the year was over, he had defeated his rival and stood at the head of the class. He had learned the lesson of the power of willingness. He must have learned it well —his name was James A. Garfield, and he later became president of the United States.

Many of life's finest achievements come because men and women are willing to go the second mile. Listless, half-hearted effort that fufills requirements only, blocks many programs and goals. What we accomplish in life depends not on what we have but on what we do with what we have. This is basic to achievement in any sphere. This is why there are so many ordinary and so few extraordinary people in the world. Most of us don't get results because we're not willing to pay the price.

Take, for instance, the difficult art of recording music. It is not easy to produce one disk that is note-perfect and also compelling in mood and emotion. Most artists are willing to accept an approximation of perfection. However, Wanda Landowska has made as many as twenty-four recordings on the harpsichord before finding one fit for release. And Arturo Toscanini took ten years, two symphony orchestras, and twenty-six attempts before he would approve his recording of Debussy's "La Mer," a twenty-three-minute work. No wonder Landowska is called the "high priestess of the harpsicord" and Toscanini the greatest conductor of modern times!

The power of willingness is responsible for much that is worth while in life. There are many hack writers who can be paid to write mystery stories for pulp magazines. Charles Dickens received no pay for his *Life of Our Lord*. Circuses employ daredevil fliers to thrill the crowds. No one hired Lindbergh to fly to Paris. Clever artists are always available to do pictures for a price. But Raphael was not paid by the hour for painting the "Madonna and Child." Goethe once asked a king to excuse him while he stepped aside to write down some stray thoughts. Later they were worked into *Faust*. Longfellow translated the *Inferno* in ten-minute periods while waiting for his coffee to boil.

In other words, some of the greatest things are done not because they have to be done, but for the love of the doing. Men are not driven to the heights. They find their way there because they can't be stopped.

Here, too, is part of the genius of the Christian faith and the hope of a better society. Seemingly impossible Christian goals are reached, simply because men have refused to take no for an answer. The objectives of the kingdom of God wait on those who are willing to give themselves to some high cause. Anything that needs to be done for the good of society can be done if men are willing.

Take the difficult matter of enlisting nurses for our church hospitals. Much is said, but little is done. An Indianapolis insurance man who had recently joined the church decided he would do something about it. His name is Edward F. Gallahue. Nobody asked him to do it. Nobody made him do it. He set about on his own to apply business methods to meet the grave shortage of nurses at the Methodist Hospital in Indianapolis. This hospital had been forced to close off wards because of lack of nurses. He canvassed young-adult groups throughout the area for prospects, building a file of over 900 interested girls. These were encouraged to serve through frequent personal and mail contacts. Scholarships were provided for those who could not pay for training. At the beginning of the next semester 106 young women entered nurses' training at the hospital. This was the largest class in years. Still larger classes were to come. The plan has been adopted by the National Board of Hospitals for use throughout the nation. Mr. Gallahue solved a difficult problem by the simple method of willingly applying the principle of a well-planned sales drive to meet a human need. It always works.

Yes, great days come for the church when ordinary laymen willingly take responsibilities and duties without being wheedled or forced. The willing life always lifts the goals of the Kingdom out of the area of daydreaming and makes them possible before our very eyes.

So it is that the section of the Sermon on the Mount that we have been considering has real meaning for us far beyond its specific intent. As is so often the case, Jesus gives a daring example to illustrate a general principle. To get caught up in the detail is to miss the point. The turned cheek, the given cloke, the second mile, all illustrate a new attitude toward life. Not many of us are made to march a mile by enemy captors. Not many of us are ever sued for our possessions. Few of us are ever slapped on either cheek. But all of us are held captive by custom and convention. Most of us are threatened by enemies of greed or laziness or selfishness. Many of us are faced with evil in the form of misunderstanding, fear, and hate. We overcome them, says Jesus, not by resisting or fighting them but by side-stepping them! We live beyond their reach or effect when we do more than is expected or required of us. We outwit our enemies by outliving them!

CHAPTER SEVEN

"Ye have heard that it hath been said, Thou shalt love thy neighbour, and hate thine enemy. But I say unto you, Love your enemies, bless them that curse you, do good to them that hate you, and pray for them which despitefully use you, and persecute you; that ye may be the children of your Father which is in heaven: for he maketh his sun to rise on the evil and on the good, and sendeth rain on the just and on the unjust. For if ye love them which love you, what reward have ye? do not even the publicans the same? And if ye salute your brethren only, what do ye more than others? do not even the publicans so? Be ye therefore perfect, even as your Father which is in heaven is perfect."
—*Matthew 5:43-48*

THE DISTINCTIVE LIFE

If ye salute your brethren only, what do ye more than others?

ONE end of the City Post Office in Washington, D. C., carries these words:

Messenger of Sympathy and Love
Servant of Parted Friends
Consoler of the Lonely
Bond of the Scattered Family
Enlarger of the Common Life

At the corresponding spot on the other end of the same building there are these lines:

Carrier of News and Knowledge
Instrument of Trade and Industry

Promoter of Mutual Acquaintance
Of Peace and Goodwill
Among Men and Nations

These are unusual inscriptions. They glorify the everyday matter of mailing a letter. They put a halo around such hardworking people as postmen. They make of the common postage stamp a thing of beauty and power. They point up the importance of good human relations that disregard all boundaries and deal with all men alike. They suggest some qualities of the Christian.

Jesus, too, was a specialist in human relations. He, too, was interested in the communications that took place among people. He was concerned with bringing people together and with bridging the barriers that divided them. His tool was love. For him love is the great "Enlarger of the Common Life." Love is the "Consoler of the Lonely" and the "Bond of the Scattered Family." But above all, love is the divine "Promoter of Mutual Acquaintance—of Peace and Goodwill Among Men and Nations."

This kind of love, said Jesus in the Sermon on the Mount, makes for a distinctive kind of human relations. It not only ties friends and families together. It extends across all boundaries. It reaches out to the hated and the unloved. It includes enemies in its scope. This was a brand new idea. There always had been plenty of love between neighbors. But Jesus called for love between enemies! Christians were to do "more than others" at this point. They were to be different in the quality of their human relations. They were to be able to love and get along with all kinds of people. Their sympathies and understanding were to be broad and generous. Snobbishness and exclusiveness had no place in their attitudes. The Christian is marked by a loving consideration *for those beyond his own crowd.*

"Love your enemies, . . . and pray for them which . . . persecute you; that ye may be the children of your Father which is in heaven. . . . For if ye love them which love you, what reward have ye? do not even the publicans the same? And if ye salute your brethren only, what do ye more than others? do not even the publicans so?" In other words, the distinctive life is the life that loves *regardless!* This can put a halo around the common people and the commonplace experiences of life. It can make us sons of the heavenly Father and carriers of the good news of Jesus Christ.

I

The distinctive life is marked by a *strange power to win friends and influence people among those who are naturally hostile and antagonistic.* The great athlete Jesse Owens was chosen by sports writers as the outstanding Negro athlete of the first half of the twentieth century. After his days of competition were over, Owens went into boys' club work among Negro boys. He said he wanted to help other underprivileged lads to take advantage of their opportunities in a free country. Coming into Chicago to lead a large boys' club on the South Side, Jesse Owens bought a building in a white residential section. It had six small flats, all occupied by white families. When the first vacancy came, the Owens family moved into the vacant apartment. They were the only Negro residents on the block. The white families did not like this. They said that their property values would go down. They showed their displeasure in many ways in an effort to make life uncomfortable for the Owens family. One irate white neighbor in particular was outraged when he found that the little Owens girl who had been going to Sunday school with his daughter was a Negro. This man ordered the Owens child off his porch one Sunday morning and sent her home crying.

Jesse Owens is a distinctive man. Instead of becoming embittered by his situation, he decided to win over his hateful neighbors by loving them. He made friends with the children and played games with the boys. He struck up an acquaintance with the irate father which became a lasting friendship. Before long the little white girl was often over at the Owens' place with her playmate. The two girls became intimate friends as they grew up together into high school. Mr. Owens improved his own property and made a beauty spot of his yard. He painted his building and installed storm windows. Soon his place was the most attractive on the block, and the white owners had to improve their places to keep up with the Negro's home. Because of this, whenever any white property was sold, it was at a profit. Real-estate values had increased, and the spirit of good will had been improved in the entire neighborhood, because a distinctive life had led the way.

It is always so. Patient understanding, sympathetic concern, and friendly love never fail to bridge gaps and heal sores between hostile people. The distinctive life has, in this kind of love, an asset of great power in solving difficult problems of human relations. "If ye salute your brethren only, what do ye more than others?"

II

The distinctive life is marked by a *willingness to co-operate for the common good with those of conflicting backgrounds and interests*. A group of bricklayers watched while one of their number laid the last of 200,000 buff bricks used in refacing the main offices of the Kraft Foods Company in Chicago. William E. Olson, construction superintendent of the company, asked for the brick. He scraped off the mortar and asked every man to sign the brick. Then, high on the scaffolding, twenty members of Local 21, A. F. of L. Bricklayers Union, scraped their names on it. Among the names were those of Michael Heneghan, Irish; Tony Cirrincioni, Italian; Tim Larsen, Swedish; William Kreutzfeldt, German; Harry Diss, Portuguese; Emil Kroschel, Finnish; John Mazerzyk, Polish; William Keele, English; Raymond Harris, Scottish; Jacob Petrenko, Ukrainian; Jack Toussaint, French; Tony Tatosian, Armenian.

After the men had all signed the brick, Olson pulled out a crumpled piece of paper. As the bricklayers made suggestions, he wrote these words:

Many men from many homelands. All Americans now. Men with different homelands, different religions, different customs have all contributed their skill toward a common goal. But as the diplomats of the world haggle over conference tables, some swear the peoples of the different nations never can solve their mutual problems. Here, all these men worked, planned, and cooperated until they had built something lasting . . . an expression of their pride in America. Perhaps in this last brick there will always be a warm flame kindled by the men who love America.

The brick and the paper are now in the executive office of the company. They are symbols of the possibilities of the distinctive life for men, for the nation, and for the world.

"If ye salute your brethren only, what do ye more than others?" The causes of human brotherhood will not be won in ivory towers. They will come to pass on the rough scaffolding of the world's common ways. It is here that the distinctive life leads out. It finds progress in co-operation instead of conflict. It seeks to build a better society on the amazingly simple idea that men of many backgrounds can and will work together for the good of all. If the walls of the world cannot be torn down, they can at least be refaced with the shining bricks of love and mutual helpfulness.

III

The distinctive life is marked by a *sensitiveness to human need wherever it may be found*. Frank's Barber Shop in the Bronx, New York, is a very ordinary place. It has three chairs but not always three barbers. Haircutting is not too prosperous a business in the tenements. The owner of the shop is Francesco Marinosci. Frank came to this country when he was seventeen. For forty years he made a bare living for himself and his family in the little barber shop. But Frank was a friendly and helpful soul and enjoyed doing things for people. During the depression he gave free haircuts to men out of work. One Thanksgiving Day he gave a party for the poor families of the neighborhood. It cost him three hundred dollars and wiped out his savings. But, he said, the children had to have something to be thankful for.

Shortly after World War II, Frank received a letter from a stranger in the little town in Italy where he was born. The letter asked for help for a family of ten who were without food and clothing. Frank and his wife talked it over. They wanted to help, but they had so little. Frank netted fifteen dollars a week from his barber shop, and his wife earned seventy dollars in a belt factory. They had three children. They decided to help with what they had. In a few days they mailed all they could spare: Twenty dollars in cash and four parcels of old clothes. Weeks later came a reply, rich in gratitude. "We all pray that God will bless the kind Americans who have been so generous." It was enough. Prayers are a good reward.

Then another letter came. Then others. Dozens of them. The word had been passed around. People seemed to think that miracles would happen if they wrote to Frank's Barber Shop, 629 Westchester Avenue, The Bronx. To make a long story short, miracles did happen. Frank and his wife made out a $25 weekly budget for themselves. The rest they used to meet the needs that came. They bought clothes from the Salvation Army. They appealed to friends. Every night they worked in the barber shop wrapping the parcels for shipment. In six years after the first letter, Frank and his wife sent 1,500 packages abroad and donated about $5,000 in cash to schools, orphanages, and churches.

There were friendly hands to help. The Irish mailman gave special service. The Jewish tailor around the corner repaired and cleaned the old clothes without charge. The Negro cobbler cheerfully fixed old shoes as his contribution. Soon the word got around, and the story became known. Then letters came from everywhere asking for help. Appeals came from France, South America, India, Egypt, China. Frank thinned out his help a little and gave to all who asked. "What difference does it make?" he asked his wife. "Italians, Frenchmen, Indians, Chinese —people are the same everywhere. If we can do something to help the poor, we must, no matter what they are."

Frank's Barber Shop became a clearance center for meeting human need the world around. As people came to know about what was going on, they gladly contributed funds and goods. The willingness of one plain man to help his fellow men *regardless* had turned into a community project. Said Frank, "People are good. It's wonderful the way they are willing to help each other."

Here, surely, is distinctive living! It is distinctive because it lovingly responds to human need, regardless of geography, race, creed, or condition of life. It is closely akin to the spirit of the Master. "If ye salute your brethren only, what do ye more than others?" It is not a matter of human helpfulness alone that Jesus is concerned about. Neighborliness among our own kind is not enough. The life that is distinctive, according to Jesus, is sensitive to any human need anywhere. This was true with Jesus himself. It is a quality of life that restores our faith in human nature and overcomes all kinds of barriers that separate man from man. This is a sure key to great living. It changes barber shops into castles. It makes of any man a citizen of the world and a resident of the Kingdom.

IV

The distinctive life is marked by *a desire to make a personal contribution to the betterment of society without expectation of return.* Most of our efforts to get along with people are selfish in motive. Most of the organized programs of human relations and public relations have some personal return in mind. But the distinctive kind of human relations that Jesus taught is of a different quality. It is the natural outgrowth of a loving interest in our brother men. In spite of our harsh exteriors most of us have soft hearts. We want to help. We would like to be of some use to someone. Jesus urged men to follow this impulse. But in it all we are to do more than others. We are not to salute our brethren only. We are to do more than write checks. *We are to give something of ourselves without hope of return.*

Harry Eva was fourteen years of age when his parents died. He was left penniless and without friends. He went from his home in Vermont to Boston to find work. But jobs were scarce in those days. His money was soon gone, and he was turned out of his rooming house. He spent night after night sleeping on benches in Boston Common. He was always cold and hungry. But he had been reared in a strict religious home, and he asked God to help him. He promised God that he would help homeless boys when he grew up. Later he found work in a café. His income was $6.00 per week plus his meals in the café. He saved four dollars out of every six toward his dream of setting up a home for homeless boys. He lived for this dream for nine years, and in that time he had saved up $400 for the project. He was determined to do something for the betterment of society *himself*.

Taking his $400 he went to New York City and rented an old store for his first home for homeless boys. He went down to Union Square and found six stranded boys. The next week he had twelve. They took turns sleeping on chairs and on the floor. He taught the boys to help one another. They all began to pray to God for help for their home.

Over fifty years have passed since Harry Eva set up his home. During that time over 46,000 boys have known that place as their home. They have, of course, moved from time to time to larger quarters. But let Harry Eva tell the rest of the story: "Today, while New York sleeps, we search the streets, parks, subways, and water fronts for the stranded boy. When we find him, we don't ask questions about race or creed, we just give him a hearty welcome, a clean bed and meals until we are able to find work for him. We are the only free home for boys in New York. Yet I have never asked for money, nor have I needed help when it didn't come."

"If ye salute your brethren only, what do ye more than others?" Here is a distinctive life at work! Any life can be distinctive! For instance, the Volunteer Bureaus operating in eighty-five cities are acting as clearinghouses for thousands of bored Americans, enabling them to give their services without pay to such work as home nursing, boys' clubs, teaching, and care for the aged. Mrs. George V. Kulchar, who helped organize this work, said, "We no longer feel a person's civic duty is fulfilled by a donation to charity. Our philosophy today is to work *with* people as well as *for* them." This is one of the secrets of a distinctive life. Thank God for these lives everywhere. They are the salt of the earth!

CHAPTER EIGHT

*"And when thou prayest, thou shalt not be as the
hypocrites are: for they love to pray standing in the
synagogues and in the corners of the streets, that they
may be seen of men. Verily I say unto you, They have
their reward. But thou, when thou prayest, enter into
thy closet, and when thou hast shut thy door, pray to
thy Father which is in secret; and thy Father which
seeth in secret shall reward thee openly. But when ye
pray, use not vain repetitions, as the heathen do: for
they think that they shall be heard for their much
speaking. Be not ye therefore like unto them: for your
Father knoweth what things ye have need of, before
ye ask him."*   —Matthew 6:5-8

THE PRAYERFUL LIFE

Pray to thy Father which is in secret; and thy
Father which is in secret shall reward thee openly.
. . . For your Father knoweth what things ye have
need of, before ye ask him.

A LBERT EINSTEIN tells the story of a
time when he was asked by a woman to
explain his theory of relativity. His answer to her question was:

Madam, I was once walking in the country on a hot day with a
blind friend, and said that I would like a drink of milk. "Milk?"
said my friend. "Drink I know; but what is milk?" I replied that
it was a white liquid. "Liquid I know," said the man, "but what is
white?" I told him that white was the color of swan's feathers.
"Feathers I know," was my friend's reply. "What is a swan?"
I replied that a swan is a bird with a crooked neck. He said,

"Neck I know; but what is crooked?" At that I lost patience. I seized his arm and straightened it. "That's straight," I said. Then I bent it at the elbow. "That's crooked." "Ah," said my blind friend. "Now I know what you mean by milk!"

So it is that many things are hard to explain. One of these is prayer. Most of us are blind in our feeble efforts to understand it. At best our wisest explanations are halting and awkward. This keeps many away from the secret chamber. However, strangely enough, we do not quit using milk simply because we cannot fully explain what it is. It is poor argument, therefore, to say that we will not pray because we do not understand the meaning of prayer.

Jesus himself demonstrated this idea in his use of prayer. He made no effort to argue or analyze the subject. Yet prayer was for him a real and vital experience. For instance, consider the section of the Sermon on the Mount in which he discusses prayer. He gives a few simple instructions about prayer and then gives the Lord's Prayer as an example. That is, he took the fact of prayer for granted as a normal part of life.

He told his hearers that prayer was not a matter of show, as it often had been made to seem in those days. True prayer was a sacred and secret fellowship between themselves and God. It was to be simple and sincere. There need be, he said, no noisy beating of the doors of heaven, since God knew already what they needed. Such prayer was not just an exercise in religious ceremony. It could be a rewarding experience. "Pray to thy father which is in secret; and thy father which is in secret will reward thee openly." The idea was not that a casual, occasional prayer would act like magic to make our dreams come true. Rather, that a prayerful life would supply the deepest needs of our personalities. We should consider three aspects of the prayerful life.

I

The prayerful life *acts as a cushion against the disturbing frictions of every day*. Here is one of our greatest needs: protection against the pressures of modern living.

Fred Allen said one time, "This insane modern civilization is too much for the Moses Model human body. Here we have an organism that was designed for Biblical times. Yet we expect it to cope with artificial lighting, executive board meetings, the din of automobile horns and soap operas, carbon monoxide, cigar smoke and bubble gum. No wonder we've all got ulcers and high blood pressure."

The multiplied irritations of life tense our nerves and exhaust our bodies. They wear us out unless we build some inner defense against them. In fact, it is hard for us to estimate the damage done by the simple frictions as well as the larger frustrations of life. Dr. Hans Selye, professor of experimental medicine at the University of Montreal, has given us some eye-opening ideas about nervous breakdowns and nervous exhaustion. He took some rats and kept them in a cage. He took good care of them, but he worried them constantly. He gave them food, but he had a dog stand outside their glass cage and growl and threaten them as they tried to eat. Loud noises were produced in all manner of ways, and heavy objects were dropped on their cage to frighten them. In a short time the rats were worn out, although they had done nothing but be disturbed!

If rats can't take it, neither can human beings. Dr. LeRoy F. Levitt, director of the psychiatric outpatient department of the Mount Sinai Hospital of Chicago, stated that at least 50 per cent of all hospital beds in the United States are occupied by the mentally ill. Said he, "A million persons in the United States are disturbed to the extent that they are considered psychotic. Five hundred thousand of these are in hospitals." He declared that any kind of severe stress can disturb the emotional equilibrium of a person to the extent that physical changes can occur. "Not only the pollen count, but also what comes over the radio or TV set, also the fact that a son or younger brother may be ill, all contribute to making us what we are."

In other words, it is of supreme importance for us to provide a cushion for the frictions of life. Prayer does this for us. Jesus told us to go into a secret place and close the door to shut the world out. He was saying that we need solitude if we are to cope with the clamor and busyness of life. We must have quiet periods of meditation when we are alone with ourselves and with God. We must take time out to give our spirits a chance to live and grow. Regular periods of prayerful solitude will prove a great boon to any life.

Said Jan Struther, "The best cure for optical strain is a complete change of focus. When the eye is exhausted from watching the inexplicable antics of human beings, clap it to a telescope or microscope: the behaviour of stars and beetles, tho scarcely less baffling, will come as a relief."

If we are to stay sane and serene, this same change of focus is necessary for the soul. Prayer is the key. The prayerful life sets up a margin of safety for the human personality. The prayer habit neutralizes the shocks of a rough and rugged world. The prayer spirit acts as a buffer between ourselves and our schedules. This is so because in prayer we surround ourselves with the infinite. We learn to live in the presence of the Eternal. In prayer, as Alexis Carrel suggests, man stands before God "like the canvas before the painter or the marble before the sculptor," and exposes his needs before the heavenly Father. This does things for us.

The French scientists Louis Daguerre and Nicéphore Niepce were the real discoverers of photography. They had caught images on sensitized glass plates but could not keep them from fading. They experimented for a long time to try to find out how to fix the image on the plate and thus take pictures. Nothing would stop the images from fading. One day in the laboratory Daguerre accidentally left some exposed plates next to a flask of mercury. Something startling happened to these plates. The images *remained fixed!* Thus the art of photography was born with the "daguerreotype."

It is so with the life of prayer. We all have occasional flashes of insight and peace. Then they are gone. But it is when we continually expose ourselves to God that the image of his goodness, beauty, and truth becomes fixed in our hearts. This exposure does something startling to us. The prayerful life gives us the calm poise of those who cannot be shaken. It sets the pattern of our life after the mind of the Infinite. It puts around the spirit a border of peace through which nothing can pass.

II

The prayerful life *helps make sense out of living*. In a world that baffles and frustrates, no need is greater than this.

Comedians seem to like to poke fun at our troubled age. This time it is the unpredictable Gracie Allen. Most of us know that Gracie has an "illogical logic," as it has been called. She makes sense of situations, but the wrong kind of sense. For instance, in one TV program Gracie put salt in the pepper shaker and pepper in the salt shaker. George asked her why she did this. Her answer was true to form. "Because," she said, "if I get mixed up, I'll be right!"

There is more to this double talk than meets the eye. Gracie is saying in her own way something that all of us feel—namely, that ours is a bewildering world and that we need some key to meet its confusion. All of us are mixed up. We need something to set things right. We must locate ourselves and find a sense of direction if we are to keep going with any degree of satisfaction and purpose. And it takes more than putting salt in the pepper shaker. No neat trick can do it. It takes the ministry of the Divine that comes only through continuing prayer.

It is not an explanation of life that we need so much as it is an orientation of our own souls. Gerald Heard put it this way:

> Our minds . . . bubble and heave, gutter and slump like a fermenting morass. . . . To resolve the ego is far more important than to solve any problems. For all human problems have their final root in the unresolved self. . . . Those who practice the Presence [of God] . . . do not expect either specific answers to temporary problems or conscious sensations of immediate blessedness. These may come, but they are byproducts. The principal [result] . . . is a change of being, rather than an increase in doing.

It is by means of this "change of being" that we find meaning and purpose in our chaotic world. When we keep God's company, we come to have something of the divine perspective. We see ourselves as the children of the Father, not as aimless bits of helpless matter. We see our world as God's world in which eternal forces are at work toward great ends. We see that suffering can bring redemption. We see the soul of man fortified by the powers of heaven in its conflict with evil. We see that truth and love through personality are the norms and standards of life. We see mind winning the age-old struggle over matter. We see the spirit of man unconquerable before the violent enemies of humanity. The prayerful life sees all this because it is in constant company with the divine Companion. It is this that enlarges our stature and establishes our status on the earth. It is this that quiets our fears and keeps us going with cheer and faith.

An amateur astronomer in Ohio by the name of Louis J. Zerbee has invented a remarkable and useful machine. It enables a navigator on a ship to establish his position without loss of time spent in making the intricate calculations that were once necessary. The navigator now locates the position of two stars and feeds the information to this machine. It then tells automatically the location of the ship within one mile. Mr. Zerbee spent seventeen years perfecting this amazing device, which is now being used by the United States Navy. It is called the Zerbee Celestial Fix Finder.

Here is a suggestive name and function for the inner secret chamber of prayer that Jesus talked about. For prayer *is a celestial fix finder!* In it our fumbling doubts and questions are resolved, and we locate ourselves as the children of God! The prayerful life enables man to find his bearings in the complicated and seemingly impersonal universe in which he lives. Prayer lifts before us goals worth striving for. It helps us chart our course and lay our plans with a sense of direction and security.

Jesus said that God knows our needs before we even ask him. We don't have to waste time in intricate, metaphysical calculations. We face toward God, and he meets us where we are. He knows we need freedom from the prisons of hate and fear. He knows we need forgiveness from the folly of our sins. He knows we need comfort in the losses of life. He knows we need support for our hopes and dreams. He knows we need guidance on life's common ways. And through our prayer he meets these needs. When we surrender before him our resentments and our desires, our pain and our despair, we find that life is good after all. The prayerful life helps us to find our bearings even though we cannot know our destination. What prayer does *for* us does not count as much as what it does *to* us.

III

The prayerful life *is a source of personal vitality.* "Thy Father which seeth in secret shall reward thee openly." Prayer for Jesus was no mere requirement of religious ritual. Neither was it a mystical route for a comfortable retreat from life. He knew that the prayer life would get results. In his own life he demonstrated the remarkable personal vitality that comes in some measure to all who live in constant and close touch with God the Father.

A deeply religious woman in a small Pennsylvania town wanted to share with others her own personal experience with the power of prayer. After much thought she did a very unusual thing. She rented five hundred billboards in the New York City subway system for an entire month. An advertising company prepared a simple sign with a plain six-word message. For a whole month blasé New Yorkers were greeted with these words along with the beer and chewing gum signs: "Prayer Changes Things—Prayer Changes You." That was all the sign said. But it was a true and terse exposition of our text.

Prayer does change things. There is much well-documented evidence of its results in history and in human affairs. For most of us most of the time, however, the message might well read: "Prayer changes things *because* prayer changes you." Prayer is no heavenly grab bag by which we grasp the baubles of life, however desirable they may be. But habitual prayer does help to make us marked personalities. In prayer we become unified inside. Prayer broadens our horizons and deepens our understanding. Through prayer we are fortified with energy not our own to aid us in the struggle of life. A rich prayer life burns out the dross and pettiness that divert our interests. It sets our minds free to attack the real business of living. Prayer sparks our outlook with buoyancy and courage. When we are thus changed, we will see things changing all about us.

To find these results in prayer, we must deal with it experimentally rather than as a dull duty. Many educators, doctors, businessmen, and scientists have in this way become advocates of prayer as a vital force making for personal growth, health, efficiency, and creative living.

For instance, Angelo Patri, widely known psychologist and authority on child rearing, has this to say about the value of prayer as a factor in education:

Prayer is the sustaining force of the spirit. It is what holds us up, strengthens us for the last effort, lifts us beyond weakness and failure. . . . Life is a battlefield from which there is no release until the end, and prayer is our greatest resource in the daily struggle. For that reason I would teach children to pray, not as to Santa Claus for gifts, but as to One who can grant us the strength that will enable us to have and to get what we need. What we need, not just what we want. Our greatest need is for spiritual strength and we get that by prayer.

A distinguished doctor, Edward A. Strecker, added the testimony of many physicians when he said:

Prayer is the language of religion; but it is also a mighty force in our daily life. . . . A doctor sees many examples of the power of prayer. . . . True prayer—by which I mean sincerely lifting your mind and heart to God—can change your life. For example, prayer has an important place in psychiatric treatment. . . . Through prayer the patient can take his troubles to God and find the support and strength he needs.

A famous businessman makes it a regular practice to have a quiet time with God as he is confronted from time to time with important decisions and difficult problems. He asks for divine insight and for God's guidance. He said, "Whenever I have practiced this method of thinking, the right answers to my problems have always come."

The scientist George Washington Carver spent up to several hours each morning alone with God before he began his labors in his chemical laboratory. He said that these periods of creative solitude led to many of his finest discoveries.

The prayerful life is a secret of personal power no man should overlook. It does not cancel our own efforts. God cannot work in a vacuum. He works through our own minds and labors. But in prayer we learn that quietness can be as creative as action. In the prayerful life our finite thinking and efforts are purified, vitalized, and directed by the infinite resources of eternal power. "Pray to thy Father which is in secret; and thy Father which seeth in secret shall reward thee openly." We are to be pitied if we turn down an offer like this!

CHAPTER NINE

"Lay not up for yourselves treasures upon earth, where moth and rust doth corrupt, and where thieves break through and steal: but lay up for yourselves treasures in heaven, where neither moth nor rust doth corrupt, and where thieves do not break through nor steal: for where your treasure is, there will your heart be also. The light of the body is the eye: if therefore thine eye be single, thy whole body shall be full of light. But if thine eye be evil, thy whole body shall be full of darkness. If therefore the light that is in thee be darkness, how great is that darkness!"

—Matthew 6:19-23

THE WEALTHY LIFE

Lay not up for yourselves treasures on earth. . . .
But lay up for yourselves treasures in heaven. . . .
For where your treasure is, there will your heart
be also.

THE St. Petersburg, Florida, *Times*, in an effort to boost circulation, one time ran daily clues to a treasure of two hundred dollars it had buried somewhere in the St. Petersburg area. On the day the final clue was printed, two thousand people gathered in front of the newspaper plant to get the first edition as it came from the presses. Twenty-five minutes later the treasure had been found on Snell Isle. In the mad scramble several things happened. Six people were injured in auto accidents. Several women fainted in the mob scene in front of the *Times* building. Four people had to be dragged out of waist-deep mud. And the crowd ripped up stakes on a building site, which had to be resurveyed. The newspaper people agreed that the stunt was a big success. The Fourth of July circulation had been upped 5 per cent!

This treasure hunt is a symbol of a popular attitude of mind. The lure of gold can become a mania. The effort to get something for nothing is a popular pastime. The search for treasure is often an all-controlling interest of life. It leads us into antics and dangers that are at the same time pathetic, humorous, and tragic.

Jesus knew this to be so. He gave a good deal of attention in his teaching to the relationship between a man and the goods of life. It was not an economic interest as such. It was a religious interest. For he saw many losing their souls by trying to depend on things to make them happy. In the Sermon on the Mount he deals with the subject in a direct and forthright way. He warns his listeners that if they put their trust in earthly treasure, they will likely lose it. He counsels them to put their faith in spiritual rather than material values. He knew that their lives would take the direction of their chief interest. And it was their lives that he was interested in. "For where your treasure is, there will your heart be also." This is one of the most familiar yet most neglected teachings of the Christian faith.

I

The things we live for determine the direction of our lives. The philosopher Spinoza said that the three things men want most are riches, honor or fame, and satisfaction of lust. H. L. Mencken gave his idea of the objectives of living when he said, "To be happy (reducing the things to its elementals) I must be: (a) Well-fed, unhounded by sordid cares, at ease in Zion. (b) Full of a comfortable feeling of superiority to the masses of my fellow-men. (c) Delicately and unceasingly amused according to my taste."

Are these the chief ends of life? Are these the things we work and struggle to achieve? We do not like to think so in our better moments. However, the fact is that for the most part men set great store on money as the central goal of life. Too often we revolve all our living around the golden treasure.

Someone has written this little ditty about stationery on the stock exchange:

The market opened with Marking Inks a black spot, while Gums and Adhesives were rather sticky. There was an absorbing interest in Blotting Papers, and Rubber Stamps created a good impression. The prices on Rubber Bands were rather elastic. Christmas, Wedding, and Birthday Cards were all cheerful, but Funeral Cards were dull. Diaries and Calendars showed a slight change over yesterday. Numbering Machines continued to alter, but Notepapers remained stationery. Embossing Presses made a good yearly impression while Sealing Wax held tight to previous gains. Account Books were a ruling feature while Stapling Presses held firm. Loose Leaf Books held together very well.

The point is, we are tempted to interpret all of life in terms of income and markets, prices and trends, profits and losses. But when we thus measure the affairs of every day in terms of their monetary value alone, we are lost in a sticky maze of black spots. When our treasure is invested in Rubber Bands and Blotting Paper or their equivalent, our hearts are likely to be elastic and absorbent objects of pettiness and greed. "For where your treasure is, there will your heart be also."

The problem with most of us is not the piling up of treasure. We find it hard enough to pay our bills and taxes and keep up our obligations to our family and community. However, we are not therefore excused from the point of Jesus' message. For Jesus is not interested in the amount of money we have, as such. He is interested in the direction of our lives and their quality. And he knew that our attitude toward material things, regardless of the amount we might have, determines the set of our souls and the richness of our lives.

The two verses following the text help explain Jesus' viewpoint toward the goods of life. The word usually translated "single" should be translated "generous." And the word translated "evil" should be "niggardly." Therefore these verses would read thus: "If therefore thine eye be generous, thy whole body shall be full of light. But if thine eye be niggardly, thy whole body shall be full of darkness." In other words, the emphasis of Jesus is not between poverty and wealth, but between stinginess and generosity! It is a key to life itself. The generous view of money and goods makes life rich and full. The grasping, niggardly outlook upon things makes us hard of heart and poor of spirit.

There are other things besides riches, fame, and lust for which men live. We can choose to live for service, for love, for freedom, for a better world. We don't have to be grubby, self-centered slaves to gold. The choice is squarely before us.

George Washington Carver was offered $100,000 a year by Henry Ford and the best laboratory money could buy. But he chose to live on his $1,500-a-year salary at Tuskegee Institute, studying peanuts. George Washington Crile, the discoverer of adrenalin, could have earned enough in one hour one day a week to live in luxury. He chose to live to bless mankind.

Each of us is controlled by some central, basic aim and drive. A person must decide for himself what this is to be. But Jesus reminds us to mark well the decision, for upon it depend the direction and character of our lives. "For where your treasure is, there will your heart be also."

II

Earthly treasure alone is an insecure basis for human well-being. "Lay not up for yourselves treasures upon earth, where moth and rust doth corrupt, and where thieves break through and steal." In Jesus' day much of the goods of life was made up of fabrics—rugs, garments, hangings. Vermin threatened these things when they were stored. Likewise, other more durable goods were not safe from thieves behind the mud walls of the houses of that time. In fact, the hoarding of wealth was a difficult thing in those days.

It is difficult today. And dangerous, too, in spite of the physical protection of steel vaults and insured bank accounts. For these things are no protection against the inroads of warped judgment and barrenness of soul that rust and corrupt those who put their trust in gold.

An eighty-four-year-old ragpicker was buried in a pauper's grave in New York after he had died in surroundings of abject poverty. City authorities later found a fortune of $500,000 in a Brooklyn warehouse vault belonging to the old man. His name was Henry Chapin Smith. He was a graduate of Harvard and had been a classmate of the poet Robert Frost and an intimate of the philosopher Henry James. Of such can be the futility of gold!

A man by the name of John Raklios was found wandering wet and alone on a rainy day in downtown Chicago. He was picked up by the police, but he could not remember where he lived. John Raklios had come to this country from Athens, Greece, at the age of nineteen with only ten dollars to his name. After years of scrubbing and saving he had started in the restaurant business. He had worked his way up to the ownership of a chain of thirteen restaurants worth four million dollars and lived in a $70,000 home. Now, old and broken, he was wandering aimlessly on the streets looking for a job as a dishwasher!

All human experience bears witness to the deceptiveness and insecurity of fame and fortune. Alexandre Dumas was the world's most prolific author. He produced nearly one hundred plays, as well as eleven hundred volumes of novels and historical romances. Moreover, he was the first writer to make five million dollars. At one time he was the most widely read novelist in the world. Yet the author of such immortal works as *The Count of Monte Cristo* and *The Three Musketeers* died penniless. Not only that, but he ended his brilliant career by compiling an ordinary cookbook!

This principle holds regardless of the level of income. When men depend on money alone for security, life has a way of folding up, no matter what the level of income. This is seen in the experience of the welfare agencies in our cities. Investigation by the courts has shown that in thousands of cases, families who have the guarantee of relief money go to pieces. Judge Jacob Panken, one of the justices of the Domestic Relations Court of New York, said, "I firmly believe a community must help care for its needy. But because I believe also in human dignity and self-respect, I am desperately worried about the 167,000 families now on relief in New York City. Every day in court I amass further evidence that our relief set-up is sapping their will to work; that it is encouraging cynicism, petty chiseling, and barefaced immorality."

Most of us are neither wealthy eccentrics nor relief rollers. Yet no one escapes the force of the message that we cannot depend on worldy goods alone for our well-being and security. The average family in the United States has an income of $3,000 a year. One half of the nonfarm families own their homes. One half of all families own cars. Three out of ten have TV sets. Six out of ten have telephones. Nine out of ten have refrigerators. Four out of ten have bank accounts and own United States Savings Bonds. We need to be grateful for such a generally high standard of living among our people. However, the fact remains that a man can be just as much of a materialist with a $3,000-a-year salary as with a $30,000 income. A car in the garage and a TV set in the parlor are no guarantee of the good life. And when a bigger car and a better TV set in a larger house become sole objects of worship and worry, we have sold our souls for a mess of pottage. Any man who trades his health and peace of mind for ulcers and a coronary disorder in a mad race for a place in the sun will live to regret it. Any man who exchanges his family's happiness for a big bank account will wake up some day to the realization that he has made a bad bargain. Greed for gold makes men gamblers, cheats, thieves, and drunkards. It is one of the greatest causes of worry and ill health. These are the moths that corrupt and the thieves that break through our best defense and steal away our treasure.

III

True wealth lies in spiritual treasure. "Lay up for yourselves treasures in heaven, where neither moth nor rust doth corrupt, and where thieves do not break through nor steal." Few of us ever have the chance to store up worldly goods. And all earthly treasure is subject to many risks. In addition to the rust and the thieves there are other dangers. These include inflation, depressions, war, floods, loss of jobs, taxation, market fluctuations, and death. But all of us may store up things of the spirit. Our true wealth is in the love and respect of our fellow men. It is in a clear conscience and a peaceful soul. It lies in the courage and faith with which we play our part. It comes as we honor God and serve our fellow man. It grows as we master ourselves in the interest of some high cause.

Jesus was interested in this kind of wealth. He wanted us to have it. He knew it would last forever and bring deep satisfactions along the way. He also knew that it could not be bought. Therefore the Master would be amazed to read this crass statement of Roman Catholic policy in the Catholic weekly magazine called *Our Sunday Visitor,* published in Fort Wayne, Indiana.

It is foolish for a Catholic to think that what he gives to the church is just so much out of his pocket. As a matter of fact, God will repay it a hundredfold. There are so many ways in which he can do so, such as keeping sickness out of the home, thus reducing physician's bills, protection of the members against automobile and other accidents, and what is more the sending of spiritual favors from heaven which would otherwise not be given.

The Protestant does not believe in this kind of spiritual treasure. The favors of God are not bought and paid for with cash. It is true that our spiritual stature grows as we give. Giving to the church is an important part of the Christian life. But we do not lay up heavenly treasure by bargaining with God. The sale of indulgences is one of the most repugnant abuses of religion ever devised. And the people who try to ease their consciences by attempting to buy their way into the kingdom of God are to be pitied.

A truer commentary on this idea may be found in Henry van Dyke's story *The Mansion*. The rich man in the story is selfishly concerned with his own interests. He builds for himself a big mansion on earth. However, when he reaches heaven, he is surprised and disappointed to find that there is only a tiny hut prepared for him. The poor man in the story is a doctor in a small community. He lives to bless and heal all those who suffer. He gives generously of himself to those in need. He lives in a modest house on the earth. And when he gets to heaven, he is amazed to find a mansion reserved for him!

But most of us are not so much interested these days in heavenly treasures after death. We want some treasure on earth. This is the point of the teaching. For Jesus' entire ministry was devoted to helping men to live the rich, abundant, wealthy life on earth. If we do this, our heavenly quarters will take care of themselves. But we are so often blind to the real nature of the wealthy life. We stand in our own way in failing to attain it. We do not see that it is of the spirit and not of the flesh.

The wealthy life is the life that is rich of soul and spacious of mind. It is generous in its judgments of others. It is sold always on the high and fine things. The wealthy life loves the free market of light and truth. It writes off wrongdoing and deceit and shoddiness. The wealthy life invests heavily in love and forgiveness and understanding. Its trend is ever onward and upward with sublime faith and resolute courage. It bears without complaint its part of the loads, losses, and burdens of life. The wealthy life is humbly grateful for the dividends of the beauties of nature and the bounties of field and forest. It stands in awe before the divine Presence in the universe. It lifts the fallen and encourages the weary. It performs the duties of life with a ready hand and trusts God when explanations are beyond reach.

These things make any life wealthy, regardless of any limiting circumstance. This is the kind of living that lays up treasures in heaven, where moth and rust do not corrupt and where thieves do not break through and steal. For these are the values that are beyond corruption and cannot be stolen. They make life rich beyond our fondest dreams.

> Sunrise and Morning Star,
> And one clear call to give,
> And may there be no clouding of the sky
> When I go forth to live.
> But such a glow, as shining seems ablaze,
> Too full for shade or night,
> When that which drew from out the sun's vast rays
> Bursts into light.
>
> Daylight and Morning Bell
> And after that to work;
> And may there be no soft and subtle spell

To make me shirk.
For though into the maze of toil and strife
My tasks may set my way,
I hope to meet my Master life to life,
As I shall live this day.[1]

<hr />

[1] William Hiram Foulkes, "Facing the Dawn. " Used by permission of the author.

CHAPTER TEN

"The light of the body is the eye: if therefore thine eye be single, thy whole body shall be full of light. But if thine eye be evil, thy whole body shall be full of darkness. If therefore the light that is in thee be darkness, how great is that darkness! No man can serve two masters: for either he will hate the one, and love the other; or else he will hold to the one, and despise the other. Ye cannot serve God and mammon."
—Matthew 6:22-24

THE UNIFIED LIFE

No man can serve two masters.

THERE is an interesting anecdote in Lytton Strachey's biography of Queen Victoria. It concerns a quarrel the queen had with her husband, Prince Albert. After the quarrel Albert locked himself in his room. Victoria knocked on the door in anger.

"Who is there?" Albert asked.

"The Queen of England," was the answer.

But Albert did not open the door. There came a hail of loud knocks. The same question and answer were repeated several times. Finally there was a pause followed by a gentle knock. "Who is there?" was the same relentless question.

This time the reply was different. "Your wife, Albert," the queen said softly. The door was opened immediately!

We are all like the queen. Each of us houses more than one personality. The same individual may be both queen and wife, angel and devil, Dr. Jekyll and Mr. Hyde. Sometimes we are ruled by our ideals, sometimes by our passions. It is this conflict that keeps us in hot water with ourselves and with our own private world. We find, however, that the closed doors of life swing wide open when our total being is held captive by the best that is in us.

Jesus warned us against the danger of the divided life, in the strong words of our text: "No man can serve two masters: for either he will hate the one, and love the other; or else he will hold to the one, and despise the other. Ye cannot serve God and mammon." This statement leaves little room for compromise for those who like to live with two faces. It says without any margin of argument that it is impossible to live a double life. In this brief section of the Sermon on the Mount, Jesus is saying, in other words, that life was made to be whole, unified, mastered by some single, dominant purpose. Otherwise it falls apart. When God is master of our life, we are then the masters of life itself.

Our text has at least three important meanings for us.

I

It means *the impossibility of moral and spiritual neutrality*. There can be no fence-sitting in our relationship to moral and spiritual values. This teaching of Jesus is not some pious doctrine which we may accept or discard as we choose. It is a law of life itself. There is no escape. Ours is a moral universe. We are forced to take sides whether we want to or not.

Much of our moral confusion comes exactly at this point. Far too many of us have shielded our own uncertainty by taking intellectual refuge in some moral no-man's land. We have thought it polite and modern and fashionable to affect a broad-minded tolerance before both goodness and evil. Robert J.

McCracken, of Riverside Church, New York, described this position when he said:

In nine cases out of ten what goes by the name of tolerance is really apathy. There are too many easy going Americans who are up in arms against nothing because they have no fixed standards of right and wrong. They do not come out positively and whole heartedly on the side of anything because, unlike their fathers, they have no robust convictions. Tolerance is a virtue, but it is not the supreme virtue.

You see, we cannot cope with life without some deep-set faiths in ultimate values. We need these more than we need food and drink and shelter.

The currently widespread idea that there is neither good nor evil—in any absolute moral or religious sense—is a misreading of human experience. For life itself is an eternal conflict between God and mammon, the good and the bad. To deny this is to be blind to the drama of history and the unending struggles of the human heart and mind. But more than this, indifference to moral values reduces life to dimensions of vulgarity and materialism.

Much of our current fiction is a reflection of the futility of this attempted neutrality. For instance, the critic Edmund Fuller has this to say about the novel *Let It Come Down* by the talented author Paul Bowles. It "is full of motion, evil, and boredom. For the book recognizes no good, admits no evil, and is coldly indifferent to the moral behavior of its characters. It is a long shrug." This is what happens to life when it is lived in an unreal, gray world, ruled by appetites but unmoved by any uplifting standard. It becomes one long shrug!

This is true because in the world of the spirit if we are not for, we are against. To refuse to take a positive stand for the right and the good, means that we are in effect supporting the wrong and the evil, whether we admit it or not. "No man can serve two masters: for either he will hate the one, and love the other; or else he will hold to the one, and despise the other." As attractive as we may think it would be, there is no middle ground. Our influence reaches up or pulls down. It never remains on dead level.

It was the operation of this principle that led, or rather drove, the famous English philosopher C. E. M. Joad from agnosticism to a positive belief in God and goodness. In his book *God and Evil* he tells how the devilish and deliberate cruelties of the German concentration camps opened his eyes to this truth. He saw there the terrifying active results of negative, neutral moral thinking. Here he saw the simple denial of goodness and God, which was at the heart of the Nazi idea, turn into "outright wicked choice, willful nihilism, perverse cruelty, [and] consent to demonism." It is always so. When we turn our backs on God, we automatically turn our faces toward anti-God. When we withhold our hands from doing good, it is not long until they are busy with evil. And it is impossible to hold such a decision in suspension, for the simple reason that life forces it upon us with every passing day.

All of this is powerful argument for the unified life. Jesus was no stranger to the passions of life. He knew something of the destructiveness of evil. He warned men not to trifle with it. He knew we could not evade one of the basic laws of human existence: "You cannot serve God and mammon." The worldly-wise cynics who are contemptuous of moral idealism had better know that moral neutrality leads to moral tragedy.

II

The text declares *the necessity of unity in personality*. Jesus' words have meaning in the realm of mind and spirit as well as in the area of moral values. The unified life is psychologically necessary if we are to live comfortably with ourselves and effectively in our world. Our very inner nature requires that we come to some unity within ourselves. We cannot live with purpose and power when our personalities are scattered and our central loyalties are divided.

To be sure, there are plenty of people who attempt to do just this. Indeed, many of us are scattered because we are the victims of a scattering civilization. This is no new problem. Here is the way a newspaper account describes the manifold influences that pull and twist us out of shape: "The present evils which afflict the country have been produced by overbanking, overtrading, overspending, overliving, overdashing, overdriving, overreaching, overcheating, overplaying, overborrowing . . . and overacting of every kind and description." This was taken from the New York *Herald* for May 3, 1837!

It may be that generations of this kind of thing are just now catching up with us. At any rate, we are told that there are 8,500,000 people in the United States with mental disorders and that half of all the patients in the country are psychiatric cases. One of the underlying reasons for these upset personalities is the strain that comes from trying to live at odds with oneself. Too many people are overliving because they are overburdened and overextended with overactivity. Divided loyalties make for frayed nerves and disturbed minds. And these things cause all kinds of mental and physical illness. They are the source also of much of our day-to-day unhappiness. The findings of the modern sciences of medicine and psychiatry are underscoring in a striking way the truth of the words of Jesus, "No man can serve two masters." For when we try to do so we are caught in the middle every time.

The continuous tension that comes with the incessant pounding of *outside* events and the thrust of complex desires *within* must be resolved. Our very happiness depends on it. Our mental health requires it. We need some one central unifying principle or philosophy or personality big enough to command our total loyalty and around which life may be built. We are lost without it. The swift tempo of the changing times, the muddle of conflicting ideas, the uncertainty of the future, demand a unified life if we are to survive.

How is this to be done? G. George Fox, a psychologist, has said that a chief ingredient of this unifying principle is "a feeling that life has a positive view; that we don't come and go without a purpose; that there is a Divine Planner who directs the universe even though we don't fathom it."

In other words, when we quit serving two or more masters and begin to serve one supreme, divine master, things straighten out for us. We discover peace instead of turmoil. We then have a chance to understand ourselves. Life ceases to be an endless series of question marks. We then have a chance to attack the puzzling business of living with some degree of satisfaction and success. This is a key that can transform life.

Many have found it so. For instance, Ray Stannard Baker described his own experience in these words:

Am I happy? Yes, I am. Once I had a civil war going on in me, and I was unhappy. Now, I know who I am and what I am trying to do. I know what life is for. It is to make better men, nobler men —and after that still nobler men. It's to throw all you are and everything you have into that one purpose. It's to understand the wonder and the truth of life—and then to make other people understand. It's to make life a great adventure—not to blink sorrow, or evil, or ugliness; but never to fear them.

Here then is the one clue to victory in the civil wars that go on inside us. If we want peace of mind and soul, we had better get us one master only: the Master! The life that is unified around God is the life that is steady and serene. The life that lives for the great and good things always holds together.

III

Our text infers *the importance of choosing and serving God as Master*. We are not the helpless creatures of circumstance or heredity. We have the power of choice. We are free beings. The argument that we ourselves have no control over the course of life is contrary to all experience. Thank God a man may choose his gods. We may *allow* ourselves to drift with the tide of events or passions. *But we don't have to!* Even in "not choosing" we are making a choice. The sovereign free will of the human mind is one of the greatest gifts of God to men. We may choose to serve mammon. We may choose to serve God. But we may choose! More than that, we *must* choose! We cannot serve both.

Jesus was well aware that there are many choices that face us. There are choices that have to do with our personal habits, our idea of success, our health, our education, our relation with others, and our pleasures. But he confronts us with only one choice, the greatest of all. "Ye cannot serve God and mammon." He was wise enough to know that our decision at this one point would affect all the other decisions of life. To be sure, some choices do not present such clear-cut, black-and-white alternatives. But it is also true that once we have established an overall, dominant direction of life toward God and the things of God, we are able to resolve our conflicts and make our minor choices with greater insight and certainty.

The word "mammon" itself actually means property. It is not always used in an evil sense. It may be thought of as representing worldliness in any of its many forms. Jesus is saying that at the central controls of life we are going to have to choose between love of God and love of gold, between the service of God and the service of things, between the worship of God and the worship of self. Far too many modern pagans want to settle for respectability or freedom or some other secondary alternative to mammon. Anything less than this basic choice of God will leave us disorganized and unhappy. Jesus knew that unless we choose to serve the eternal God, we will be at the beck and call of a thousand earthly masters.

The life and work of the French author André Gide, who died in Paris at the age of eighty-one, is an example of such unresolved conflicts. He was torn between his puritan boyhood and the hedonism he found in North Africa. His homosexuality was in conflict with his love for his wife, Emmanuèle. His emancipation from convention fought with his search for a personal substitute. His artist's ego was at odds with his social conscience. He himself said that he was "compelled" to write about his own inner conflicts, which "otherwise would have fought constantly with each other."

But to escape such conflicts by writing about them is an endless and fruitless treadmill. André Gide found it to be so. The same is true of escape by reading, traveling, drink, work, the spending of money, or any other secular activity. It takes more than any of these. We need some ultimate and final master. And we find this only as we choose God. Nothing less will do. It is then that the diverse elements of life become fused into one unified whole. It is then that the confused chaos of existence takes on shape and form and order. It is then that we have a chance for genuine joy and creative activity. When we choose God, we put a roof over our scattered souls.

The experience of Philip Cabot, a Harvard graduate and the son of a notable family, demonstrates the effect of such a shift in the center of gravity of life. The strong crosscurrents of his affairs had driven him to the brink of a physical and moral breakdown. His doctor ordered him to give up his business and to take the rest cure. On the verge of despair he went to the seclusion of his camp in the Connecticut Valley. He took along a stack of detective novels to read. These soon bored him. He quite casually began to glance through *The Meaning of Prayer* by Harry Emerson Fosdick, which someone had given him. He became fascinated and absorbed. He said:

It seemed that in worship, or prayer, and in my Bible, the solution to the riddle of my universe had been revealed to me; for I was living in a new world of peace, beauty, and gladness, such as I had never conceived. . . . That condition has continued, except that I have returned to the world of men to take up again my daily chores with the keenest interest and with a sureness of touch and an absence of worry and excitement, and my health has continued to improve in a remarkable way.

Philip Cabot discovered the beauty and power of a life unified in the reality of God. This may be for us, too, the solution of the riddle of our own particular universe. For, you see, *"no* man can serve two masters."

CHAPTER ELEVEN

"Therefore I say unto you, Take no thought for your life, what ye shall eat, or what ye shall drink; nor yet for your body, what ye shall put on. Is not the life more than meat, and the body than raiment? Behold the fowls of the air: for they sow not, neither do they reap, nor gather into barns; yet your heavenly Father feedeth them. Are ye not much better than they? Which of you by taking thought can add one cubit unto his stature? And why take ye thought for raiment? Consider the lilies of the field, how they grow; they toil not, neither do they spin: and yet I say unto you, That even Solomon in all his glory was not arrayed like one of these. Wherefore, if God so clothe the grass of the field, which to day is, and to morrow is cast into the oven, shall he not much more clothe you, O ye of little faith? Therefore take no thought, saying, What shall we eat? or, What shall we drink? or, Wherewithal shall we be clothed? (For after all these things do the Gentiles seek:) for your heavenly Father knoweth that ye have need of all these things. But seek ye first the kingdom of God, and his righteousness; and all these things shall be added unto you. Take therefore no thought for the morrow: for the morrow shall take thought for the things of itself. Sufficient unto the day is the evil thereof."   —Matthew 6:25-34

THE TRUSTFUL LIFE

Seek ye first the kingdom of God, and his right-eousness; and all these things shall be added unto you.

—Matthew 6:33

BASIL KING in the opening chapter of his book *The Conquest of Fear* made a classic statement about fear when he said:

When I say that during most of my life I have been the prey of fear, I take it I am expressing the case of most people. I cannot remember a time when a dread of one kind or another was not in the air. In childhood it was the fear of going to bed, later it was the fear of school, still later it was the experience of waking in the morning with a feeling of dismay at the amount of work that had to be done before night. In some form or other fear dogs every one of us. The mother is afraid for her children, the father is afraid for his business, most of us are afraid of our job. There is not a home or an office or a school or a church, in which some hang-dog apprehension is not eating at the heart of the people who go in and out. I am ready to guess that all the miseries wrought by sin and sickness combined would not equal those we bring on ourselves through fear. We are not sick all the time. We are not sinning all the time. But most of us are always afraid—afraid of something or somebody.[1]

Jesus knew well this universal plague of fear. He was witness to the blighting effect of fear on the minds, bodies, and personalities of men. Many times he spoke on the subject. He had the only real solution to the problem of fear. It is no psychological trick. It is complete trust in God. Jesus yearned to so establish men's faith in a loving, powerful, trustworthy God that they might escape the ill effects of care and worry and fear. This prescription is beautifully put in the ten verses of the Sermon on the Mount of which our text is the key. Jesus speaks of God's care for the birds, lilies, and grass. He reminds his listeners that they are more important than these. He assures them that if they put God first, all needful things will be added. And he concludes with the assurance: "Take therefore no thought for the morrow: for the morrow shall take thought for the things of itself. Sufficient unto the day is the evil thereof." There are at least three aspects of this trustful life which will make it both possible and meaningful for us.

[1] Used by permission of the publishers, Doubleday & Co., Inc.

I

The trustful life *is based on an acknowledgment of God's provision and care for our needs.* These ten verses are related to the preceding section of the Sermon on the Mount, which deals with our relationship to things. Jesus knew that men's passionate desire for the goods of life is in turn a primary cause of worry and fear. When we depend on things for support, we lose our sense of need for the support of God. A modern proof of the extent of such fear was seen in the result of a Gallup Poll in the spring of 1952. Field reporters put this question to a representative cross section of men and women living in all parts of the country: "What would you say is your biggest worry these days—the thing that disturbs you most?" Nearly half the answers, 45 per cent, said that money was the source of the chief fears of life. This was the number-one worry. The number-two cause of worry was the threat of future war, which was listed by 21 per cent of those polled. In other words, more than twice as many people are worried about material things than about war. And this in one of the most prosperous periods in the nation's history. Money and the future are responsible for 66 per cent of our worries! It is no wonder that Jesus sought to release men from the grip of this deeply rooted enemy of faith.

He did so by assuring them of the greatness and providence of God. As evidence of this, Jesus cites the fact of God's care for his creation. Even the birds of the air are fed, the flowers of the field are clothed, and the lowly, perishable grass is not forgotten. Jesus points out that if God takes care of these humblest objects of his creation, he surely will not fail man, the highest. "Therefore take no thought, saying, What shall we eat? or, What shall we drink? or, Wherewithal shall we be clothed?" In all of this, Jesus is making the point that God, having given the gift of life, will likewise sustain it. "Is not life more than food?" Jesus asked them. That is, if they became unduly exercised about the *means* of life, they would miss the *meaning* of life itself.

In these passages Jesus in no way argues against work or planning or saving. He does not speak for idleness or slothfulness or neglect of responsible and thrifty living. These things show a false idea of trust. The key to his message is found in the Revised Standard Version translation of the phrase usually translated "take no thought." It is more accurately translated, "Take no anxious thought," or "Do not be anxious" (R.S.V.) Its strongest meaning is, "You must not be distracted by cares." This phrase is repeated five times in these ten verses. Instead, then, of our text reading, "Take therefore no thought for the morrow," it should read, "Therefore do not be *anxious* about tomorrow." Likewise the reading is, "Do not be *anxious* about your life, what you shall eat." "Why are you *anxious* about clothing?" "Which of you by being *anxious* can add one cubit to his span of life?" (R.S.V.) That is, anxiety and worry are totally unproductive!

To be sure, we must take thought about food, clothing, health, and the future, but we must not let them become the goals of life. If we do, they will become a burden to the soul, and we will be fretful and anxious and fearful. How is this to be avoided?

The answer is both simple and profound. "Seek ye first the kingdom of God, . . . and all these things shall be added." The goal of life is to know God, to love him, and to trust him. Then we can never be distracted by the cares of earthly living. The fact is that such a trust requires a bigger idea of God than most of us have. Our God is a great God. He is the creator and sustainer of our universe and of all universes. He is the God of the humanity of all history. He causes the seeds to multiply and the sun to shine and the seasons to roll. He establishes laws of nature and life beyond all our understanding. He stores the earth and the sea with an abundance of all things for all men forever and ever. He abides with his children for generation after generation with unceasing faithfulness. He clothes the earth with majesty and glory. This is our God, a God strong enough and big enough to take care of us. "Shall he not much more clothe you, O ye of little faith?" We can trust him because he is trustworthy!

II

The trustful life *requires a sense of detachment from the disturbing events of time.* The Revised Standard Version reads: "Therefore do not be anxious about tomorrow, for tomorrow will be anxious for itself. Let the day's own trouble be sufficient for the day." Jesus here does not ignore or deny the existence of trouble, present or future. He admits it. He does not say that we should not face seriously the problems of life. What he is saying is that troubles can best be met by our dealing with them one at a time. He is saying that God will give us the measure of strength needed for the troubles of tomorrow when they come, just as he does for those of today. He is saying that the man whose trust is in God protects himself from the ill effects of worrisome events by the possession of a divinely ordered margin of safety. When we live with God, we can afford to live day by day, because we have a divine buffer between us and the disturbing events of today and tomorrow. It is when we borrow trouble from the future that we are unfair to ourselves and to God.

In other words, the man who trusts God is *in* the world but not *of* it. He is subject to time but not a victim of it. He has a heavenly perspective which enables him to detach himself from the endless stream of events in order not to be hurt by them. It is as Sigrid Undset put it in "The Cross": "When man comes up on a height above his native place, and looks down from it to his own dale . . . he knows each farm and fence, each thicket, the gully of each brook; but he seems to see for the first time how these things all lie on the face of the land." Even so, he whose chief business is God's business, removes himself from the lowland of his tribulation to a vantage point on the hills. From there he sees the events of the day in their true setting and knows that life does have order and purpose.

It must be insisted that this sense of detachment, which is part of the trustful life, does not mean isolation from the responsibilities and pain of living. To use our heads is no betrayal of our trust in God. There are those who think it is religious to live in some fool's paradise of sweetness and light. They long to bask in some secluded philosophical never-never land away from the heat and burden of the day. They blame everything that happens on God, when often their own stupidity should be blamed. They resent the intrusion of the sound and fury of everyday troubles. They would like to be immune to the agony of the world. But this is impossible, in spite of the teaching of some religious sects. Jesus never interpreted life this way. He made no retreat from the struggle. He never denied the presence of evil. He did something far more spirited and challenging than that. He kept his life within the focus of the providence of God. He lived by and for eternal values even in the midst of the ever-changing ways of earth. In the words of George A. Buttrick, "Jesus conquered worry by keeping his eyes and mind on life's main business. . . . In this faith many troubles can be met and mastered. Sickness can be turned into sympathy, and sorrow into insight." The question marks remain, but their sting and bitterness are gone.

Our detachment from the disturbing events of life grows out of our attachment to the things of God. When we venture to live for the things that are really important, we discover so much that is unimportant. No angry circumstance can break for long the serenity of him who lives the trustful life with Christ in God.

III

The trustful life *implies a willingness to follow the guidance of God*. It is at this point that the trust relationship between man and God most frequently breaks down. We who have faith in God need also to learn to trust him. This is not easy, for too often we want our way instead of being willing to seek and find and follow God's will for our lives. In this section of the Sermon on the Mount, Jesus challenges us to give our lives and affairs in complete surrender to the heavenly Father. This is the one sure and final cure for worry and care. It is also a certain source of personal power and peace. Then it is that we can know the meaning of the message of the Master when he tells us that tomorrow will take care of itself without our worrying about it.

This is the counsel of strength, not of weakness. It is a means of self-fulfillment, not self-distrust. The principle was put quaintly by an old Egyptian sage in these wise words: "The boatman reacheth the landing, partly by pulling, partly by letting go; the archer striketh the target, partly by pulling, partly by letting go." So it is. The reason we worry so much about the future is that we ourselves push and pull too hard and too continuously. We strain and fret and torment ourselves over *our* plans and *our* hopes. We need to let go sometimes and let God take over. We need to adjust our plans to his master plan. We need to take advantage of the psychological forces of action and reaction. We need to know that personal achievement does not come by human effort alone always applied in one direction. It comes rather as our human powers are supplemented by divine directions and resources.

Carl Erskine, star pitcher for the Brooklyn Dodgers, learned this technique the hard way, as most of us do. After a brilliant start in the majors, he failed and was farmed out to the minors. He discovered that his thinking had been as much at fault as his pitching arm. He had pushed himself too hard. He had feared failure too much. He had worried too often about his future success. When he finally returned to the Brooklyn team, he had learned a profound secret of living and working without fear. He had learned to work in partnership with God. Speaking of his experience, Carl Erskine said:

Once back in the majors again, the big question was: "Could I stick?" I began to concentrate much more on positive thinking. My prayers before a game now are not for victory, but that I be in tune with God's way. If my mind gets a sense of rhythm and coordination, my body does too. Confusion and pressure then bother me less. If I neglect this meditation—call it an "inside pitch"—my mental conditioning is not complete.

We neglect this "mental conditioning" at the risk of being stalled by the confusions and pressures of life. But when we discover its possibilities, we will never pitch a game without it. We find it when we pray not for what we want but for what God wants. We find it when we pray not for success or health but that God may use us for his purposes. We find it when we pray not for the absence of struggle but for strength to struggle for the will of God. We find it when we pray not for an easy and comfortable future but that God may be our companion whatever the journey.

When we do this, we will be immune to the poison of worry and fear. We will then be able to stand on our own feet knowing God will never let us fall. We will then know without question that if we take care of today, God will take care of all the to-morrows.

In his memoir of his wife, Ramsay MacDonald told of her death in these words:

Her faith stood the test to the end. When she knew that she was close by the opening gateway of death, I asked her if she desired to see any one who would speak to her of what was to come. "That would be a waste of time," she replied. "I have always been ready. Let us praise God together for what he has been. He has been very good to me in giving me my work, my friends and my faith. At the end of the day I go gladly to him for rest and shelter." She was convinced that life and time were not the sum and substance of experience, and went away as though but starting on a journey which, beginning in darkness, would proceed thru light. She would hold my hand, she said, till those who had gone before gave her greetings.

Of such is the trustful life. "Seek ye first the kingdom of God, and his righteousness; and all these things shall be added unto you."

CHAPTER TWELVE

"Judge not, that ye be not judged. For with what judgment ye judge, ye shall be judged: and with what measure ye mete, it shall be measured to you again. And why beholdest thou the mote that is in thy brother's eye, but considerest not the beam that is in thine own eye? Or how wilt thou say to thy brother, Let me pull out the mote out of thine eye; and, behold, a beam is in thine own eye? Thou hypocrite, first cast out the beam out of thine own eye; and then shalt thou see clearly to cast out the mote out of thy brother's eye."

—Matthew 7:1-5

THE UNDERSTANDING LIFE

Judge not, that ye be not judged. For with what judgment ye judge, ye shall be judged: and with what measure you mete, it shall be measured to you.

JAMES THURBER once said, "The human species is both horrible and wonderful. Occasionally I get very mad at human beings, but there's nothing you can do about it. I like people and hate them at the same time. I wouldn't draw them in cartoons, if I didn't think they were horrible; and I wouldn't write about them, if I didn't think they were wonderful."

Most of us feel somewhat the same way. In our better moments we are sure that people are wonderful creatures. The trouble is that we have too many dark moments, when it is easy to find fault with our fellow men. It is impossible, of course, to keep from passing day-by-day judgments of one kind or another on other people. This is a normal, everyday experience with everybody. We all have our likes and dislikes. The processes of an ongoing society depend on such judgments and decisions. Furthermore, we cannot remain neutral when faced with moral questions. As Christians we are at times called upon to evaluate people and to condemn wrongdoing and wrongdoers.

In this passage of the Sermon on the Mount, Jesus is not objecting to such judgments. He is, rather, lifting before us a severe warning against self-righteous severity in our personal dealings with our brother men. He appeals to us to be merciful and generous in our attitudes toward our fellows. He urges us to avoid the censorious spirit. He encourages the understanding life.

The principles set forth in these five verses form a fundamental basis for Christian human relations. The operation of these principles will revolutionize our personal lives and the life of society. Indeed, here is a simple key for happier lives and a better world. "With what measure ye mete, it shall be measured to you again."

There are at least three principles in this teaching which Jesus surely wanted to bring to our attention.

I

Human judgments are limited. A young reporter was instructed by his editor never to state anything as a fact that he could not verify from personal knowledge. Soon afterward he was sent out to cover an important social event. Many prominent and important people were present. The story the reporter sent in read like this: "A woman giving the name of Mrs. James Jones, reported to be one of the society leaders of the city, is said to have given what purported to be a party yesterday to a number of alleged ladies. The hostess claims to be the wife of a reputed attorney."

Something of this kind would be a good discipline for many of us when we are given to passing critical judgment on others. The plain truth is that we often say a lot of things we simply do not know anything about. It is surprising how little we actually know about the people we discuss so freely. We are all too willing to condemn people on rumor or gossip or on insufficient information. Indeed, the louder we condemn, the less we sometimes know. The critical spirit grows on us if we are not careful. It makes us boors and bores. We find considerable satisfaction in blanket condemnations of everyone and everything. For instance, we may even approximate the orator who spoke of John Jay, who helped negotiate the peace treaty with England in 1783, in these bitter words: "Damn John Jay. Damn everyone who won't damn John Jay. Damn everyone who won't put lights in his window and sit up all night damning John Jay!"

Jesus was well aware of this perverse streak in human nature. In this passage he is warning us not to fall into such a trap. He is implying that human weakness is universal, that we are all subject to judgment. He suggests that the self-righteous soul who delights in picking flaws in others will thereby be exposing his own. He is saying that harsh criticism is usually based on lack of complete evidence. He is pointing out that our own limitations and likes and dislikes make it difficult for us to assess accurately and fully the limitations of others.

Here is Thomas Carlyle's estimate of Charles Lamb: "A more pitiful, rickety, gasping, staggering, stammering Tomfool I do not know." On the other hand, this is what Henry Hazlitt said about the same Charles Lamb: "The most delightful, the most provoking, the most witty and sensible of men."

It is a good thing that the final judgment is in the hands of God and not ourselves or our brother men!

This habit of passing snap judgments on people without sufficient evidence is not only unfair. It is dangerous. It can blot character. It can destroy reputations. It can raise dark questions that are hard to live down. It can involve innocent parties. Busy tongues can be instruments of the Devil.

The understanding life recognizes that there are in every doubtful situation many factors that do not appear on the surface. The Christian hates evil. But he is loath to believe it about people. He is always willing to make allowances for the frailty of human nature. He is willing to admit his own ignorance of the facts when faced with the temptation to pass some hard judgment. For he knows that he will be judged with the same judgment. When we do not know, we ought to keep still.

II

Human censure is self-condemning. This is the sharp point of this message of the Master. Jesus not only warns us against ill-considered criticism of others. He says that it works damage on ourselves. "Judge not, *that ye be not judged.* For with what judgment ye judge, *ye shall be judged:* and with what measure ye mete, *it shall be measured to you again.*" These are strong words. There are no qualifying ideas to soft-pedal the stern action of the law of retribution. Jesus is saying in no uncertain terms that we will be judged in the same way that we choose to judge.

There is a positive side to this principle, of course. Jesus underscores this later in the Golden Rule. In this present passage, however, it is the dark side of the idea that is up. We get back from life what we give to it. When we are spiteful, life treats us spitefully. When we are hypercritical, life has a way of going sour on our hands. Sharp tongues betray an inner weakness and show us to be immature Christians.

Indeed, there are those who say that anything evil or unkind we do to others is always paid back in kind. The repayment may be indirect and delayed, but it always comes.

A dramatic example of this law of retribution is told by Carl Wallace Petty. In 1911, when an epidemic of streptococcus pneumonia was depopulating vast areas of north China, a friend of Dr. Petty called on a wealthy New Yorker and asked for a contribution to help send medicines, nurses, and doctors to the suffering Chinese. The man refused. He was sharply critical of the whole idea. He thought the Chinese ought to take care of themselves. A few years later an outfit of Chinese laborers on the way to dig trenches in France was billeted on Long Island for several months. They had scarcely sailed for the western front before the epidemic called influenza broke out in New York City and swept through the nation. The Chinese plague had come to America by those laborers. And one day Dr. Petty read in the paper that the daughter of the rich New Yorker who had refused to help the Chinese had died in the clutches of the Chinese influenza!

"With what measure ye mete, it shall be measured to you again." There are many who will not agree that the operation of this principle is as sharply defined as that. But it is true nonetheless. It is supported by many passages in the Scriptures. "Whatsoever a man soweth, that shall he also reap." "They that take the sword shall perish with the sword." "He that soweth to his flesh shall of the flesh reap corruption." "He that doeth wrong shall receive for the wrong which he hath done; and there is no respect of persons." "Be sure your sin will find you out."

It is a law that is likewise true in human experience. "Water finds its own level sooner or later, and our treatment of others returns at last upon ourselves." Its effect may not be dramatic or automatic. But quietly, subconsciously, and inevitably, the way we treat our fellow men reacts upon our own outlook, spirit, and effectiveness as human beings. Frederick D. Maurice put it this way: "Looking [in other people] for the faults, which

I had a secret consciousness were in myself . . . has more hindered my progress in love and gentleness . . . than all things else."

Modern psychology says that it does a great deal more than this. Our attitudes of anger, hatred, and chronic faultfinding actually poison the mind and body. Our grudges and our sustained ill will have an unhealthy reaction on the nervous system. The unkind word, the sly innuendo, the unfair judgment, all leave a residue in the souls of those who give them. There is a plain truth here that cannot be avoided. Life is made up this way. If we cheat, we will be cheated. If we deceive, we will be deceived. If we lie, we will be lied to. If we misuse our authority over others, we will pay for it. If we condemn falsely, we will be falsely condemned. If we live at odds with other people, we will be at odds with ourselves. "With what measure ye mete, it shall be measured to you again." Here is a law that is as impersonal and inescapable as the law of gravity. We do well to understand and use it. Ralph Waldo Emerson put it this way:

A man cannot speak but he judges himself. With his will, or against his will, he draws his portrait to the eye of his companions by every word. Every opinion reacts on him who utters it. It is a threadball thrown at a mark, but the other end remains in the thrower's bag. Or, rather, it is a harpoon thrown at the whale, unwinding, as it flies, a coil of cord in the boat, and if the harpoon is not good, or not well thrown, it will go nigh to cut the steersman in twain, or to sink the boat.

III

Human understanding begins at home. In the next three verses Jesus puts the responsibility for the understanding life right where it belongs: on the individual heart and conscience. He asks us in plain language why we worry about other people's faults and don't do something about our own. Granted that a great many people have a great many faults. So do we! He says it is absurd for us to try to improve our fellow men when we make no effort to improve ourselves. "Thou hypocrite, first cast out the beam out of thine own eye; and then shalt thou see clearly to cast out the mote out of thy brother's eye." Here is a solid basis for human understanding and constructive concern. When we are conscious of our own limitations, we are never so quick to pin ugly labels on our fellow men. As the old spiritual put it,

> Not my brother, but it's me, O Lord,
> Standing in the need of prayer.

This may well be a theme song for many of us!

An unknown writer brings this matter down to earth by listing ten good things for which no one has ever been sorry. "1. For doing good to all. 2. For speaking evil of no one. 3. For hearing before judging. 4. For thinking before speaking. 5. For holding an angry tongue. 6. For being kind to the distressed. 7. For asking pardon for all wrongs. 8. For being patient toward everybody. 9. For stopping the ear to the talebearer. 10. For disbelieving evil reports."

These things sound simple and commonplace. But they are hard to do! It is much easier and quicker to cover up our own deficiencies by holding up to scorn the weaknesses of others. In fact, sometimes our effort to correct the shortcomings of others is a defense mechanism. It gives us a feeling of superiority to compensate for our own inner faults which we are unwilling to face and correct. The people who are always eager to correct someone else are likely to be in need of some correction themselves. We are too quick to believe the worst about other people. We are too unwilling to give them the benefit of the doubt.

Human understanding begins at home. The words usually translated "mote" and "beam" are more accurately rendered "splinter" and "log." It is an obvious use of sharp contrast to make a point. Jesus seems to be saying that the faults which we often criticize in others are small and insignificant compared with our own bigger sins of pride or prejudice, self-righteousness or hypocrisy, which lead to the criticism. We like to point with scorn at sins of the flesh when we ourselves are much more guilty of sins of the spirit—sins of envy, jealousy, intolerance, prejudice, egotism, and lack of love. With these major impediments to our sight, we cannot see to judge our neighbor's shortcomings. We need to concentrate on getting rid of these primary sins of our own lives. When we can see with the eyes of love, we will find that most people are a great deal better than we thought they were.

This principle has wide application to the life of today. Said Eric Johnson, "We talk about building bridges of brotherhood around the world in answer to the communist pretensions, and that's a splendid vision. But brotherhood begins on a man-to-man basis at home and not on a man-to-man basis across the oceans. Without that footing it is idle talk and an empty vision." The understanding life breaks down social barriers by the simple process of friendly acquaintance. This begins with individuals on both sides of the fence.

The way this idea operates was demonstrated one time in the little town of Sonoma, California. Freddie Wing was for many years the Chinese chef at the Swiss Hotel in Sonoma. He saved his money, joined the United States Army, visited China, and returned with a bride. After the birth of a son, Freddie bought a $12,000 house in the all-Caucasian Hillview section of town. When he moved in, he sent out two hundred invitations to a housewarming, including all his neighbors. There were two hundred acceptances, including the mayor, both bank presidents, and General Hap Arnold's widow. They all had a fine time together. Said Freddie Wing, "These people are my friends." Said a neighbor, "We are proud of Freddie here."

Only on some such personal basis of human understanding will our so-called social problems be solved. When we get the log of prejudice and fear out of our own eyes, we discover the insights of love. And we find that the limitations of our neighbors are, oftentimes, only insignificant splinters.

CHAPTER THIRTEEN

"Give not that which is holy unto the dogs, neither cast ye your pearls before swine, lest they trample them under their feet, and turn again and rend you. Ask, and it shall be given you; seek, and ye shall find; knock, and it shall be opened unto you: for every one that asketh receiveth; and he that seeketh findeth; and to him that knocketh it shall be opened. Or what man is there of you, whom if his son ask bread, will he give him a stone? Or if he ask a fish, will he give him a serpent? If ye then, being evil, know how to give good gifts unto your children, how much more shall your Father which is in heaven give good things to them that ask him?"   —Matthew 7:6-11

THE ADVENTUROUS LIFE

Ask, . . . seek, . . . knock.

THE American author James Branch Cabell believed that life is a tiresome thing with disillusionment as its only reward. Speaking of hard-won success on earth, Cabell said he saw "only the strivings of an ape reft of his tail and grown rusty at climbing, who has reeled blunderingly from mystery to mystery, with pathetic makeshifts, not understanding anything, greedy in all desires, and always honeycombed with poltroonery." It is no wonder Mr. Cabell felt that the only way to make life bearable is to retreat into romantic dreams.

Many modern people feel the same way about the business of living. All the zest and lift have gone out of life. They barely manage to exist day by day, victims of a deadly routine. Living for them has become a melancholy and materialistic matter of toiling, eating, lusting, and sleeping.

Is this the true nature of man? Is life futile, after all? Is the end of all our strivings to be a blank wall and an empty dream? There are many things to make us think so. Life has a way of beating us down with little to pick us up. Is there any formula to save us from discouragement? Is there a method that will bring to life the precious quality of enthusiasm?

Jesus offers exactly such a prescription in the Sermon on the Mount. It is found in the familiar words "Ask, and it shall be given you; seek, and ye shall find; knock, and it shall be opened unto you." There is magic in these words but not in the usual pat understanding of them. The secret lies in the nature of the Greek verbs, "ask, seek, knock." These are in the present tense in the original. This means that they denote *continuing* action.

Thus, the reading of this passage means, "*Keep on* asking, and it shall continue to be given you; *keep on* seeking, and ye shall keep on finding; *keep on* knocking, and it shall continue to be opened unto you: for everyone that keeps on asking keeps on receiving; and he that keeps on seeking keeps on finding; and to him that keeps on knocking it shall continue to be opened." In other words, the adventure is in the seeking, not in the getting!

With this fresh reading of these familiar words in mind, suppose we look at some of the qualities of adventurous living that mark the Christian.

I

The adventurous life *welcomes the high climb.* We all recall that a scientist one time said that the chemical elements in a human body had a market value of ninety-eight cents. Today researchers tell us that the atoms in a human body have an energy potential of 11,400,000 kilowatt hours per pound. This is worth

$570,000,000, or a total of $85,500,000,000 for a 150-pound man! Thus nuclear physics joins the Christian faith in putting an infinite value on human life! We are literally billionaires. No wonder Jesus called to men to "Ask, . . . seek, . . . knock," and to keep on asking, seeking, and knocking. Why should we not dream and aspire and set our faces toward the stars? We are the children of God! We have the right to look up beyond the horizons of the possible. To reach up beyond ourselves is not only our right; it is our obligation! To refuse to do so is to deny our own nature and to betray the God who made us in his image.

There is a reason why so many of our goings and comings seem like the "strivings of an ape reft of his tail." It is that we have lifted before ourselves no great challenge. A survey has shown that nine out of ten persons have no definite plan in life. They are just coasting along. This is not in keeping with Jesus' idea of living. Too many people try to coast along in their Christian experience and program. This is to go downhill. Human personality is bigger and better and finer and happier only when we are strongly and continuously held by some godly ambition. We are meant for struggle and for climbing! That is the way God made us. No man is worthy of the kingdom of God who turns back when the going is tough.

The American industrial leader Henry J. Kaiser said one time in a lay sermon:

Your plan for work and happiness should be big, imaginative and daring. Strike out boldly for the things you honestly want more than anything else in the world. The mistake is to put your sights too low, not to raise them too high. The definite, far-away goal will super-charge your whole body and spirit; it will awaken your mind and creative imagination, and put meaning into otherwise lowly, step-by-step tasks you must go through in order to attain your final success.

Likewise, the common life of mankind is made richer and stronger because men have dared to respond to the "high calling of God." The history of human achievement is a witness to the truth of this principle of the Master: "Ask, . . . seek, . . . knock." Roentgen aimed high, and his discovery of the X ray blessed mankind. The Curies followed a shining light, and radium has brought healing to millions. The Wright brothers sought to conquer space, and the world has become a neighborhood. Lincoln caught a lofty vision, and a race was freed and a nation united. Luther broke from tradition, and new faith emerged to bless the earth. Marconi answered a high call, and the world turned into a whispering gallery. A future world of peace and brotherhood waits on men who are unafraid of hard, lonely, and dangerous trails.

It is important, therefore, that we keep this quality of our adventuring in a day when security is a watchword. The modern American Christian will want to say with Dean Alfange:

I do not choose to be a common man. It is my right to be uncommon—if I can. I seek opportunity—not security. I do not wish to be a kept citizen, humbled and dulled by having the state look after me. I want to take the calculated risk; to dream and to build, to fail and to succeed. . . . I prefer the challenges of life to the guaranteed existence; the thrill of fulfillment to the stale calm of utopia.

Here is the modern echo of an ancient call: "Ask, . . . seek, . . . knock." This is the adventurous life! The noblest achievements and deepest satisfactions of life are strangers to those who are spiritually lazy.

II

The adventurous life *keeps reaching for things that cannot be reached.* "Keep on asking, and it shall continue to be given you; keep on seeking, and ye shall keep on finding; keep on knocking and it shall continue to be opened unto you." When we climb an upward way, we will find that the effort itself brings new and unexpected opportunities and values as we go along, even if the goal itself is never reached. Few really worthwhile things are ever handed to us. We get them by seeking them. We find them by growing into them. We can't have them unless we prepare ourselves to receive them. And if we do reach a goal, we had better set another one quick!

Dr. Liston Pope, Dean of Yale University Divinity School, tells about a certain man who had retired from business. When this man was asked one time what he did in his spare time, he said, "When I get up in the morning, I read the obituary column in the newspaper. If my name isn't there, I go back to bed!"

This is true, in effect, of a good many of us long before time for retirement. We stop growing. We are satisfied just to be alive. But life was made for more than this. We must keep on growing or we die inside. We need to be fired by the idea that today's task is but a prelude of things to come. No life need be lived on a dead level. New challenges and opportunities are forever before us. Only as we keep on learning and keep on growing and keep on knocking and asking and seeking do we find the rewards of insight and understanding and power that God has for us. Man was made to grow mentally and spiritually. To refuse to do so is to betray your own soul. Growth in Christian character and happiness is impossible unless we use the resources of worship and prayer and set our hands to the tasks of the Kingdom. We never arrive; we must always keep climbing!

Dr. Malcolm Buckley, a prominent patent attorney of New York, says that about forty thousand of the fifty thousand new patents issued every year are only improvements on ideas already patented. Yes, there is always room for improvement! Take the electric light. Twenty-five years after Edison in 1880 had made his first lamp, a new filament was added which lifted the efficiency of lamps by 25 per cent. In 1911 a new rugged metal filament made for still greater efficiency. In 1912 new chemical "getters" reduced bulb blackening and made small-sized globes possible. In 1913 came the gas-filled lamp. In 1915 the coiled filament was redesigned so as not to sag, and this improvement gave the bulb longer life. In 1919 the bulb was made tipless, and this reduced breakage. In 1925 the glass bulb was frosted on the inside instead of on the outside. This frosting gave diffused light.

It is so with life itself. No life is perfect. Strangely enough, we are all subject to improvement. We have to keep experimenting, changing, growing, if life is to follow the pattern of God. When we stop breaking new ground, life goes stale. This is true in every phase of experience. In 1910 the name Pierce-Arrow alone was valued at a million dollars. But the company did not keep pace with new developments in the automotive industry. Later, no car manufacturer would have the name at any price. The company was forced out of business because it refused to grow, and it could not even give away the name! Unless we grow, we fail! God wants us to fulfill the full potential of life. As our minds and souls and personalities expand and develop in the direction of the plan and will of God, life remains a thrilling and creative adventure. "Ask, . . . seek, . . . knock." No finer prescription for personal growth has ever been given. For the child of God needs always to be confronted with something always beyond his reach. Otherwise our faith grows cold, and life grows stale.

III

The adventurous life *is a demanding program.* Lifelong asking, seeking, and knocking demand bold hearts and stout spirits. The higher prizes of life come only to those who sacrifice for them.

The things that come to us free are often not worth having. The Christian shuns the sure thing and the easy way. He does not believe in the jack-pot lure of getting something for nothing. The high winds and the rough waters are a challenge to his skill. In the service of the heavenly Father he is willing to pay the high cost of living as a Christian. In doing so he finds life victorious, no matter what the outcome. For God always rewards the brave souls that beat no retreat and make no excuses. He rewards them with self-respect, personal integrity, and the exaltation of spirit that comes to those who master themselves.

Take the case of Ike Skelton, Jr. He was stricken with polio as a young boy. A Kansas City doctor told the parents, "If he gets better, healing will come from a higher Power than I." Months and years of painful recovery followed. Seeing Ike's determination and spirit, the doctor changed his mind. He said, "Never have I seen such a will to win."

Five years later, a student at Wentworth Military Academy, Ike was on the track team. In the big meet of the year he ran the two-mile race. His legs had recovered, but his arms were still helpless. For the race his teammates taped his useless arms to his side. In the last lap Ike sprinted down the course. It made no difference that his opponents had already finished two laps before. He gritted his teeth and tore across the line into the arms of his teammates. Said one, "The rest of them came in first, but they didn't beat that boy!"

The fact is, of course, that he who matches the challenges of life with character and courage is never beaten. Whatever the earthly outcome, he is always rewarded with the approval of God. For this no one can have any regrets. It is so in the Kingdom, too. The demands of the hour are terrific. But the challenge always is to our will to win! Without it we are lost. With it we triumph!

IV

The adventurous life *never gives up.* "For every one that keeps on asking keeps on receiving; and he that keeps on seeking keeps on finding; and to him that keeps on knocking it shall be opened." It is the *keeping on* that counts!

The psychologist Murray Banks said, "While the physiologist believes old age begins at twenty-eight, which is when physical deterioration sets in, creative imagination, the real life surge of humanity, only reaches complete development in the forties. Artists do their best work at fifty, doctors at fifty-four, jurists at fifty-seven."

The fact is, however, that many of the world's greatest creative geniuses have done their best work after sixty-five. Indeed, the adventurous spirit lasts as long as life lasts if we never give up. Robert Louis Stevenson's book *Weir of Hermiston* breaks off in the very middle of a sentence, written on the morning of his death. Sir Walter Scott began *The Siege of Malta* a few weeks before he died. Charles Dickens left *The Mystery of Edwin Drood* unfinished. Joseph Conrad was in the midst of one of his most promising novels, *Suspense*, when he passed away.

This is the way men should live their lives, full and useful to the very end! The adventurous life looks down every turn in the road with eagerness and hope. It never gives up. If one thing will not work, something else will. If one plan must be discarded, better plans appear. Far too many of us have been defeated because we gave up too soon. Plain, common, ordinary perseverance is an important part of God's plan for life. God cannot use quitters. Those who start on the Christian way and give up ought to be ashamed of themselves. God expects more of us than this.

In 1925 Harold Byrd was a consulting geologist in Brownwood, Texas. He decided he would try to dig an oil well for himself. He drilled fifty-six wildcat dry holes before he had a producer. Few men are willing to try fifty-six times in any effort. But on the fifty-seventh try a gusher came in, and Mr. Byrd later became one of the wealthiest men in the Southwest. Henry Ford worked up 871 successive models before he was satisfied with the final design for his first tractor. In 1882 seven Merritt brothers tramped the Mesabi Range in Minnesota looking for iron. They were sure, from the way their compasses acted, that the metal was somewhere. But they looked for ten long years before finding it. And then, in 1892, the discovery came as their wagons mired down in some rusty red mud.

This is the story of the spirit of man. The tireless search of the soul for God is always rewarded. The verses following the text tell us that God is on our side in our search for the good things of life. In these verses Jesus says that no father gives his son a stone if he asks bread, or a serpent if he asks a fish. So God gives good things to those who keep on asking for good things. In other words, we get what we go after. If we don't ask much of life, we won't get much in return. If our lives are a never-ending search for the rich things of the spirit—peace, love, faith, hope, joy—we can't help finding them. When the prayer of our lives is for God and the spirit of godliness, we can't fail. God himself guarantees the success of our venture. Life for the Christian is neither blind alley nor endless treadmill. The nature of the universe itself is ordered in favor of those adventuring spirits who turn their faces endlessly toward God, asking, seeking, knocking, forever.

CHAPTER FOURTEEN

"Therefore all things whatsoever ye would that men should do to you, do ye even so to them: for this is the law and the prophets." —Matthew 7:12

THE REWARDING LIFE

Therefore all things whatsoever ye would that men should do to you, do ye even so to them: for this is the law and the prophets.

IN his *Conversations with Eckermann,* Goethe once said:

Transplant Mont Blanc at once into the large plain of Luneburg Heath, and we should find no words to express our wonder at its magnitude. Seek it, however, in its gigantic home; go to it over its immense neighbors, the Jungfrau, the Finsteraarhorn, the Eiger, the Wetterhorn, St. Gothard, and Monte Rosa; Mont Blanc will indeed still remain a giant, but it will no longer produce in us such amazement.

It is like this with the Golden Rule. This one verse stands quite alone in the Sermon on the Mount. It is a kind of towering climax of the entire discourse. Taken apart from their context, these few words still remain one of the great landmarks of the human spirit. They form perhaps the most widely known and used verse of scripture in the Bible. Yet, taken in their lofty setting in the Sermon on the Mount, they seem to be a natural part of the spiritual scenery. And it is in this setting, among its lofty neighboring peaks of religious insight, that the Golden Rule needs to be interpreted. Taken out of context, it can become a mound of mere humanistic expediency. It is, on the contrary, a towering religious idea. For it is based on the Master's teaching of the dignity and worth of man as a child of God. We must keep this background in mind as we seek to discover its meaning for us.

In the Revised Standard Version the Golden Rule is stated: "Whatever you wish that men would do to you, do so to them; for this is the law and the prophets." No matter how it is simplified, these words still form a sublime and universal law of behavior and of brotherly human relations. If we had the faith and fortitude to follow such a law, we would have a key to a life of rich rewards.

In this Golden Rule, Jesus seems to be saying at least three things.

I

A positive approach to people gets the best results. It is well known that the idea of this Golden Rule was not original with Jesus. It is found in many earlier religious writings. In Judaism it reads this way: "What is hateful to you, do not to your fellow men. That is the entire Law; all the rest is commentary." In Brahmanism it is stated like this: "This is the sum of duty: Do naught unto others which would cause you pain if done to you." In Buddhism the same principle is given as follows: "Hurt not others in ways that you yourself would find hurtful." Taoism puts a like idea in these words: "Regard your neighbor's gain as your own gain, and your neighbor's loss as your own loss."

These are all negative approaches to human relations. Jesus filled the idea with a new and positive content. This made it a powerful tool of human development. Jesus was never on the negative side of life. He constantly warned men against the destructive influence of hate and fear and anger and doubt. He wanted men to approach the business of living with faith and trust and hope. Religion for him was never a matter of restrictive duty or careful creed. It was a commitment of life. It was an acceptance of the universe. It was a matter of doing and believing and being and giving. Moses had a law. Confucius had a system. Buddha had a principle. The Stoics had a philosophy. But Jesus had a life, an ideal instead of a code, an art instead of a set of rules. It is this that transforms human existence and fills it with exciting possibilities.

In the Golden Rule, Jesus is applying this ideal of positive living to the area of human relationships. He says it works like magic in getting along with other people. He says we must be for people and not against them. We must build them up and not tear them down. We must give them status, make them feel they count for something. Jesus is saying that we must have faith in men and expect the best from them. He says we need to recognize and respect the personalities of other people and not try to exploit them or take undue advantage of them. He wants us to try serving their needs in the spirit of constructive comradeship.

Why do all these things? Because they get better results than hate or deception or antagonism or suspicion or force or self-seeking. Life is smoother and easier and more productive. This may sound stuffy and commonplace. Yet, as Harry A. Overstreet puts it in his book *The Great Enterprise:* "The great enterprise of life is to create life that is friendly to other life." It is an enterprise that pays off in rich dividends of happier homes, more peaceful communities, more profitable industries, and deeper personal satisfactions.

Our world sadly needs this wisdom. We have excelled in mechanics, and we have been deficient in learning the arts of living together. A survey of 4,400 people who had lost their jobs showed that the main lack was not in skill but in comradeship. E. Stanley Jones said he found over the telegraph office windows in India this sign: "Please show the same courtesy here as you would like shown to you." Commented Dr. Jones, "They can't even run a telegraph counter without applying the Golden Rule."

Robert Whitney, president of National Sales Executives, calls this principle of the Golden Rule the "best selling principle I know." He says:

Look at it selfishly if you want to. The fact is: the more you give, the more you receive. Thinking of others pays off. . . . Once the formula is tried we've found the selfish attitude doesn't last for long. There's something about the very nature of "giving" that changes men, brings to them a sense of contribution, a sense of peace and satisfaction. It is to be found in the builders of the future—in the leaders of men—it is the true reward.

In this positive approach to people, therefore, Jesus is suggesting a formula of great power. As we undergird people with confidence and praise and encouragement and generosity, we find ourselves repaid a thousandfold. This is good psychology. It is good public relations. It is good economics. It is good Christianity.

II

We get back from other people the kind of treatment we give to them. This, of course, is the heart of the Golden Rule. Jesus is saying that we ourselves determine the way others are going to treat us. Most of us don't believe it. We like to blame others for our own trouble. Nevertheless, we largely write our own ticket. We can get any kind of returns we wish. Our rewards will be great or small depending on the size and nature of our investment.

There are those who look with suspicion on rewards as an incentive to religion. Jesus did not think that way. He was no

Spartan himself. And his chief concern was that men learn to live so as to get the most out of life. Indeed, the entire Sermon on the Mount is keyed to this idea. The Beatitudes hold out rewards for certain qualities of life. They climax with the promise "For great is your reward in heaven." Later in the Sermon he says, "For if ye love them which love you, what reward have ye?" Again, speaking of giving alms, he declares, "And thy Father which seeth in secret himself shall reward thee openly." He uses exactly the same words twice later in reference to secret prayer and again in speaking of fasting. Just before the statement of the Golden Rule he promises us we will get what we ask and seek, saying, "How much more shall your Father which is in heaven give good things to them that ask him?" *Jesus taught a rewarding gospel!*

Nowhere is this idea of reward more applicable, more observable, or more easily tested than in the matter of our everyday human relations. The Golden Rule is much more than a bit of prudential human wisdom. It brings into sharp focus a pattern of human behavior built by God into the very structure of the human family. We are not to use it in some mechanical and superficial way. We are the children of God, and lovingkindness is a divine quality, to be sure, regardless of the return. Yet, it is good to know that Jesus himself taught that love of others is no dreary spiritual exercise performed in a vacuum. It is a human, friendly thing that brings rewards.

Take the case of Lou Reese, of Scio, Ohio. In the depression year 1932 Lou bought an abandoned pottery plant at a sheriff's sale in that little town of 1,400 population. He then owned eleven cents and owed nearly $20,000. He and seven other penniless pottery workers who had been on relief started to work. They lived in the plant to save money. Lou and those who worked with him did wonders with the plant. He treated all employees as members of the same family. They were not unionized, because they received higher wages and more benefits than the union asked. The minimum wage was one dollar per hour for unskilled labor long before the unions thought of it. In addition, generous bonuses made income high for the 850 employees. Needless to say, there were no strikes. In fifteen years the company grew from nothing to a business of four million dollars a year, the second largest whiteware pottery in the country.

Then came the fire which completely demolished the plant. There was no insurance because the nature of the plant made rates prohibitive. It seemed that a bright dream had come to an ugly end. But the next day after the fire all the employees and the entire population of the town turned out to help Lou Reese rebuild. They offered to loan Lou Reese their savings. They cleared the debris of the plant. They salvaged the unbroken pottery. They worked without pay to restore the building. Even steel companies, supply houses, and railroads offered Lou Reese special concessions to get the plant going again. It was all a living demonstration of the Golden Rule. Lou Reese treated his employees fairly, honestly, and generously. He got back in return the same kind of treatment. They all prospered. It never fails.

We may expect back from other people the kind of treatment we accord them. Like so many of the sayings of Jesus, this one is true not because he said it; he said it because it is true. God rules. The universe is good. It is part of the nature of human life that, in the long run, with all due allowance for human perversity, we get back what we give. If we deal with good will, we will get good will in return. If we are friendly, we will have friends. If we forgive, we will be forgiven. If we trust, we will be trusted. If we are understanding, we will be understood. If we are generous, we will find generosity flowing back to us. This is the rewarding life.

III

Our own well-being depends on the well-being of our fellow men. We are all the children of God. We are all related in some way to one another. We are all indebted to others in ways we can never repay. When others suffer, we suffer. When others prosper, we prosper. This fact gives wide dimensions to the operation of the Golden Rule. It means more than simple person-to-person relationships. It means that no one can live for himself and to himself. It means that we must try to bring to others the same quality of life we want for ourselves.

The trouble is that our own self-centeredness stands in the way of our own happiness. Thornton Wilder in *The Bridge of San Luis Rey* tells how the old Marquesa longed for the love of her daughter with a selfish and possessive yearning. She sought it as a tribute to herself. When her daughter's love was withheld, the Marquesa became cynical. She believed in the goodness of no one. Said the author, "She saw that the people of this world moved about in an armor of egotism, drunk with self-gazing, athirst for compliments, hearing little of what was said to them, unmoved by the accidents that befell their closest friends, in dread of all appeals that might interrupt their long communion with their own desires."

No wonder she saw others in that black light! It was a reflection of her own self-centered heart. Parents need to know that their own well-being is wrapped up in the well-being of their sons and daughters. We can't get until we give. When we smother them, we are smothered.

The Golden Rule works in family relationships. It works also in economics. A leading economist of India, Professor Thomas of Madras University, put it this way: "To keep your neighbor poor while you rise in wealth is now unsound economic policy; for without a corresponding rise in your brother's purchasing power, you will yourself be hit, whatever may be your business. India is the biggest demonstration of this truth."

It works in our everyday life as citizens of a democracy. No one can live to himself in our modern, interdependent society. Each of us reflects the character and quality of the common life. If this is good, we all benefit. If it is dark with injustice and sour with evil things, we are all sufferers thereby. The Golden Rule can help make it clean and fair. Said Dorothy Thompson:

This is what the American Way of Life still means to me. It doesn't mean a 300-billion-dollar national income, or the statistics of production, or being the "leading world power." It doesn't mean "the world's highest standard of living." It means the most human standard of life and relationships; it means hard work—even, if it comes to it, austerity. It means belonging to a nation of friends, and doing as you would be done by.

The Golden Rule works, too, in industrial relations. It is good business. Recently the American Institute of Management suggested ten precepts which, if followed, would make for the manager's success. The first was, "Does he try to live by the Golden Rule?" Many modern business institutions are demonstrating the plain truth that production and profits and morale increase as employees are treated as partners in the enterprise. After ten years of polling workers, Elmo Roper concluded that their four chief desires are security, a chance to advance, treatment as human beings, and dignity. The simple recognition of these things by thousands of companies, large and small, is the basis of a widespread modern industrial revolution. At long last the human factor, and not technics alone, is coming to be the primary concern of business. Management and labor are finding that their interests are not contradictory. What is good for one is good for all. This is the American answer to the Communist hope for permanent class warfare in this country. And it is all based on the operation of the Golden Rule.

S. F. Shattuck, Vice-president of Kimberly-Clark Corporation, a large paper-manufacturing concern, said,

I am conscious of the constructive, almost religious, attitude prevalent in business today. Industrial management is evolving into the attitude of social trusteeship. This concept is spreading through the industrial life of America. Christianity has infiltrated industry, making the principles of "good business" the evidence of God's laws for men. Many a leader today whose Christianity used to be vapid now sees his faith as a trust and a way of life. Our only sure defense against disintegrating forces is a God-conscious spirituality. Regardless of whether this new day in American industry stems from Christian sources or not, the fact remains that Christianity is furnishing American business with the philosophy and techniques of a "better way." Good business is good Christianity! [1]

Here, then, is a simple, workable, practical, down-to-earth expression of Christian human relations. Our glib familiarity with the Golden Rule must not dull the luster of its possibilities. It is a magic key to the solution of many of our human problems. It makes life a rewarding experience for every man who puts it to work with the help of God and in keeping with the Christian spirit.

---

[1] *The Christian Century*, April 8, 1953. Used by permission.

CHAPTER FIFTEEN

"Enter ye in at the strait gate: for wide is the gate, and broad is the way, that leadeth to destruction, and many there be which go in thereat: because strait is the gate, and narrow is the way, which leadeth unto life, and few there be that find it." —Matthew 7:13-14

THE DISCIPLINED LIFE

Because strait is the gate, and narrow is the way, which leadeth unto life.

CÉBES, a disciple of Socrates, said, years before the time of Jesus, "Seest thou not a certain small door, and a pathway before the door, in no way crowded, for only a very few travel that way, since it seems to lead through a pathless, rugged, and stony tract? That is the way that leadeth to true discipline."

Centuries later another scholar, Walter Phelps Hall, professor of history at Yale University, gave his idea of the most important lesson of human history in these words: "The rock bottom thing about life is to keep on going when we don't want to keep on going, and to be willing to give up what isn't necessary."

So it is that the long experience of the race is witness to the truth of the memorable words of Jesus about the strait, or narrow, gate and the wide gate and easy way. It is a universal teaching that applies to all life. Like so many of the teachings of the Sermon on the Mount, it is a terse summing up of a law of life—a law that is as true today as in the time of Socrates. There is nothing particularly theological about it. It does not take a Yale professor to learn its truth. It is a simple, hard, cold fact of life that is written large on the face of every day.

Discipline of mind. Discipline of heart. Discipline of work. Discipline of sacrifice. Discipline of character. Discipline of soul. These are the narrow doors that lead to the wide-open areas of free and abundant living. Yet few are willing to enter in thereat. The easy and undisciplined ways are much more attractive. Many need no persuasion to take them, only to find too late that they lead to destruction.

There is deep meaning in this message for us and for our generation.

I

Human progress depends on disciplined minds. The slow, tortured trail of human progress is blazed by men and women who have passed through the narrow gate of the disciplined mind and will. No advance in human well-being has ever come full-blown down some broad thoroughfare. No undirected mob has ever permanently served the cause of humanity. The ideas and plans and programs that have lighted the long road of history have been born in travail, sacrifice, and devotion to the exacting discipline of truth. Whether the field be medicine or mechanics, statesmanship or science, religion or the arts, the story is the same. We see it in operation today.

Take, for instance, the matter of measurements. The narrow gate has become exceedingly narrow with man's conquest of his universe. There was a time when this gate was measured by yards and feet and inches. But it was not enough. Today mercury light waves are used. The Bureau of Standards had a roll of gold foil inserted in an atomic pile. After a year of intense neutron bombardment, one five-hundredth of an ounce of gold was transmuted into an isotope of mercury which had never existed in visible amounts—Mercury 198. This form of mercury then gives off light of such uniform wave length that its waves can be used to measure an object within one billionth of an inch. That's a narrow gate!

Take the matter of the nature of light. There was a time when we were satisfied with the use and enjoyment of sunlight in its natural form. Not any more. First its nature was studied in the ordinary spectrum made as light was sent through a prism of glass. That's still not enough. Now scientists are studying the spectrum thrown by a "diffraction grating." The latest one of these was made for the Los Alamos atomic laboratory. It has 211,000 lines crowded into a space seven inches long, more than 30,000 lines to the inch! These lines are the same distance apart with a tolerance of one millionth of an inch. The machine that draws these lines on a piece of glass operates in an underground room cut into solid rock so as to be completely without vibration. This is another narrow gate!

The world is full of narrow gates. It takes disciplined minds to go through them. The uncaring and the unheeding will never see them. The pancreas glands of pigs, for instance, were destroyed as being useless until someone came along and discovered insulin. Now the glands from 7,500 pigs must be processed to get a single ounce of insulin. Certain rocks were trampled over for centuries before men found uranium in them. Now 2,500,-000 tons of rocks are processed to get four tons of uranium. Once sea water was just taken for granted. Now scientists are recovering magnesium salts from the ocean and using them in making steel, rubber, and ink. One cubic mile of sea water gives up five million tons of magnesium salt. Narrow gates, all!

Exacting discipline is a stern requirement of our scientific age. Disciplined minds have brought us a long way from the broad, wide ways of our ancestors. Indeed, careless, haphazard thinking leads to destruction in our modern world. It takes a disciplined mind and hand to drive a jet plane or a high-powered car. And, by the same token, it takes disciplined minds to create a society that will survive in such a time.

There are other narrow gates that mark the progress of men. They are those of human brotherhood, co-operation among the nations, recognition of the rights and dignity of the common man. Few men or peoples find them. But they must be found, for they lead to life—to survival and progress and human happiness. The broader ways of hatred and war and exploitation lead down to certain destruction. Never has this been so plain as now.

It takes disciplined minds to discover these gates, minds free from prejudice and tradition and minor loyalties of creed of class. Minds disciplined by science must also be disciplined by the word of God. For love and justice and goodness are as exacting in their requirements as an electronic calculator. Disciplined consciences, disciplined emotions, disciplined homes, disciplined ambitions, disciplined education—we must not be afraid of these narrow gates. They are the sure route to man's salvation.

II

Personal achievement requires disciplined effort. This is an old, old story. Yet with our new ideas of group security we have discounted it. We have tried to protect men from the stimulus of privation. We have looked with suspicion on the ambitious, hard-working individualist. We have given our children the reins of a free and easy way of learning without self-restraint. We have glorified the safe job and the minimum effort. We have played down the old-fashioned idea of sacrificial toil and difficult goals. But these ideas we have thus emphasized are the wide gates that lead to disillusionment and mediocrity. A generation of immature, neurotic adults can be the result.

For the fact remains that the route to personal achievement and fulfillment is guarded by the narrow gates of self-disciplined effort. This was always so. It is so today. It is true in every field of human endeavor.

Take music. In the biography *Life and Letters of Peter I. Tchaikowsky*, the author, John Lane, tells of the strict self-imposed discipline it takes to be a composer. He says that the compositions would never have come had the composer waited for inspiration alone. Says this biographer, "He found that he must go to his desk each day and do something, the best he could, just to get out some music. Then in time and quite unexpectedly, rich musical ideas would come pouring into his head faster than he could write them down." Narrow gates!

Take sports. The American Tennis Association's national junior-singles championship is held at this time by a little Negro girl by the name of Lorraine Williams. Lorraine is thirteen years of age. She lives on the Chicago South Side, where she was born and reared. It is an area high in juvenile delinquency. There are eight children in Lorraine's family. Her mother is a widow, supporting the brood by working as a beautician. By all accepted standards Lorraine had no chance. There was no money for tennis rackets when Lorraine first became interested in tennis at the age of six. So she made her own out of some scraps of plywood picked up at a cabinet shop. She put up a rope across the back yard, found an old tennis ball, and went to work. Years of intense practice followed for this hard-working youngster. Her uncompromising determination and disciplined effort brought Lorraine Williams to the point where the experts predict she will be one of the top-ranking stars of the tennis world. Narrow gates!

It is a far cry from Peter I. Tchaikowsky to Lorraine Williams. But the principle is the same. It holds in every field of human endeavor. Even preachers do not escape!

Dr. Charles E. Jefferson, for thirty years the distinguished pastor of Broadway Tabernacle in New York City, was a preacher of great native gifts. But he also had the will to discipline his powers. He said one time to a group of theological students,

Gentlemen, write. Write out in full at least one sermon each week. In addition, write articles on all sorts of subjects. You may never get them published but the writing will do you good. It will keep the cobwebs out of your mind. If you do not like to write, write anyhow. If you find it painful to write, write nevertheless. If it kills you to write, make yourself do it. Blessed are they who die in the Lord.

Yes, and blessed is the man who *lives* by the laws of the Lord! The laws of life as they bear on our success as persons are clearly marked by God. They are the laws of self-renunciation and self-restraint. They carry with them the obligations of self-sacrifice and devotion to duty. They imply self-imposed disciplines of sustained effort and directed energy. These are the narrow gates through which we must go if we are to achieve our full possibilities as the children of God. To enter them, we must forsake the broad, wide-open ways of self-indulgence that lead to destruction. The pampered soul is a stranger to great living. We must give up if we are to get.

III

Spiritual growth comes only from disciplined character. Here, of course, is the heart of Jesus' message about the narrow gates. Spiritual discipline is the door to spiritual power. Moral discipline is the gateway to spiritual growth and maturity. It cannot be otherwise. Yet, it is strange that men will recognize the operation of this law in other fields and ignore it in this basic area of personality itself. The fact remains, however, like it or not, that moral and spiritual growth exact rigorous demands of self-sacrifice, purity, honesty, prayer, forgiveness, and loving service. Not many of us are willing to give what it takes. This is why there are so few saints in the world. And it is why the broad, easy, comfortable way is crowded with conventional pilgrims.

To be sure, not many of us are interested in becoming saints. But this idea holds as well for the attainment of mature, responsible living with some chance for happiness and self-respect. The trouble is that too many modern sophisticates have tried to deny the law of the narrow gates. We have been told that we should live without moral restraints. We have been urged to express ourselves freely, unhampered by spiritual ideals. Otherwise we would become the warped victims of some horrible frustration or guilt complex.

As a result we have a crop of overmature children and of overchildish adults. Unable to deal with reality, and overcome with boredom, they take to drink or sex or drugs for escape. An example is the group of teen-age drug addicts described in the novel *Flee the Angry Strangers* by George Mandel. They are a neurotic lot. "Plagued with guilt-edged insecurities, they have one fear, themselves; one foe, reality; one condition, despair; one refuge, dope." Dixie Lattimer, the heroine, aged eighteen, just escaped from the reformatory, finds relief from a sordid and sinful life of debauchery and crime in repeated shots of Heroin. In her doped-up wisdom she gives her creed: "There's nothing. There's nowhere. Everything is empty. . . . Nothing itself in a uniform of gold, and Nothing loomed bigger than Anything ever could hope to be." Toward the end the author feebly suggests that psychoanalysis may save her yet. But, as one critic put it, "Dixie and her friends may need analysis; they need spunk and a spanking more."

That's what a lot of people, young and old, need who find life empty. We need a spanking more than we need psychoanalysis! And we don't need to be dope addicts to find life empty. Lives without self-discipline are empty. Lives without God are empty. Lives without moral purpose are empty. Lives without the anchorage of religious faith are empty. Lives that are afraid to hold their own passions and desires firmly in the grip of a God-supported will are empty. We need to know that the broad, wide way of moral indifference leads to destruction, not to happiness. *Self-denial and not self-indulgence is the key to self-mastery.* We are able to stand on our feet and meet the realities of life face to face with power to overcome only as we travel the way of the narrow gates. It's not Heroin we need. It's faith in God and the stern disciplines of Christian character. These are what make life full and satisfying.

There is a special meaning in this message of the Master for the training of children. For the disciplined life begins early in the discipline of home and church. Said an unknown author:

I must not interfere with any child, I have been told; to bend his will to mine, or try to shape him through some mold of thought. Naturally as a flower he must unfold. Yet flowers have the discipline of wind and rain, and though I know it gives the gardener much pain, I've seen him use his pruning shears to gain more strength and beauty for some blossoms bright. . . . It seems to me that only weeds unfold naturally.

There is no more important or rewarding task than to shape

the mind and character of a child after the mind and character of Christ. This takes pruning and guidance and discipline in Christian conscience and Christian ideals. We have to *be* disciplined ourselves before we can learn self-discipline. These are narrow gates, but they lead to life that is mature, rich, and everlasting.

CHAPTER SIXTEEN

"Beware of false prophets, which come to you in sheep's clothing, but inwardly they are ravening wolves. Ye shall know them by their fruits. Do men gather grapes of thorns, or figs of thistles? Even so every good tree bringeth forth good fruit; but a corrupt tree bringeth forth evil fruit. A good tree cannot bring forth evil fruit, neither can a corrupt tree bring forth good fruit. Every tree that bringeth not forth good fruit is hewn down, and cast into the fire. Wherefore by their fruits ye shall know them. Not every one that saith unto me, Lord, Lord, shall enter into the kingdom of heaven; but he that doeth the will of my Father which is in heaven. Many will say to me in that day, Lord, Lord, have we not prophesied in thy name? and in thy name have cast out devils? and in thy name done many wonderful works? And then will I profess unto them, I never knew you: depart from me, ye that work iniquity." —Matthew 7:15-23

THE GENUINE LIFE

Not every one that saith unto me, Lord, Lord, shall enter into the kingdom of heaven; but he that doeth the will of my Father which is in heaven.

MOUNTAIN CLIMBERS tell us it isn't getting any easier to climb Mount Everest. A Swiss expedition which got within nine hundred feet of the top reported that, because of movement in the earth's crust, the peak is getting higher every year. According to the Swiss leader, the world's highest mountain, which used to be 29,002 feet, had already reached 29,610 feet and was still growing. He recommended that "anybody who wants to reach the top better hurry." Not long after, a British party took his advice and made it!

It is about like that with the Sermon on the Mount. Its high peaks lure us on and keep us climbing. But the higher we go, the farther away seems the goal. It is not easy to reach the top. Few of us will. But if we are to get even within hailing distance of it, we had better hurry to get started and keep going.

This last elevation, at the end of the Sermon, is the highest and hardest of all. It may be placed beside an earlier word: "Be ye . . . perfect, even as your Father which is in heaven is perfect." The section begins by warning us against false religious leaders, but the clear meaning of the teaching applies to all who would be representatives of the Christian idea. Jesus faces us with the heroic challenge *to be as good as we claim to be*. He points out the simple natural law that good fruit comes only from good trees. He declares that unless our lives match our professions, we are not fit for the Kingdom. This is stern stuff. It smokes out our shallow hypocrisies and weak alibis. It calls for a high degree of genuineness in those who would follow the Christian way.

In his autobiography, *Adventures in Two Worlds*, A. J. Cronin says, "Could we but put in practice the Sermon on the Mount, all the problems of our poor tortured universe would be solved, all the difficulties, apparently insuperable, which confront mankind would melt like the mist before the rising sun." Is this an idealistic peak impossible to climb? Perhaps. But we can at least set our faces toward its summit and keep the goal of Christlike living ever within the focus of our ambition. We can begin by living a genuine life.

I

The genuine life *is free from hypocrisy*. Jesus was always sympathetic with sinners. He was always scornful of hypocrites. Jesus loved the humble of spirit. He was indignant toward those whose goodness was a blind to hide a mean or proud heart. Jesus forgave the penitent wrongdoer. He condemned those who were clean on the outside but dirty on the inside. "Not every one that saith unto me, Lord, Lord, shall enter into the kingdom of heaven; but he that doeth the will of my Father which is in heaven." In other words, Jesus meant business. He had no patience with those who were loud in declarations of faith that were empty of supporting action.

The problem of the hypocrite has remained to this day. Helena Huntington Smith made a survey in which she tried to learn why people did not go to church. The results were published in one of our national magazines. Here was the reason a lawyer gave for not attending church: "I grew up in a small town. Two of the most crooked businessmen in town were [officers] of my church. That made me decide church people were a bunch of hypocrites." It is true, of course, that two hypocrites should not condemn an entire congregation, much less the church as such. The lawyer, like many other people, drew a conclusion from far too little evidence. However, the fact remains that plain hypocrisy is one of the most damaging blights on the Christian enterprise. One of our keenest thinkers put it bluntly when he said, "Mere profession of a Christian life does more harm perhaps than undisguised wickedness."

The trouble is that our present-day tolerance of evil and our over-all acceptance of surface respectability make hypocrisy an easy and common experience. It is much simpler to cover up than to clean up. Indeed, fakery is usually difficult to detect. The Municipal Museum of Amsterdam held a "Fake and Genuine" exhibit of art masterpieces. Fake copies of the originals were hung side by side with the genuine paintings without any distinguishing labels. Visitors were asked to try to detect the genuine from the false. Only 7 out of 1,827 visitors were able to do so! So in life. We may be able to fool others by our false fronts. But the fact remains that a pious appearance is no guarantee of the real article.

The genuine Christian is a living example of the Christ spirit in every department and area of life. He is Christian through and through. He is Christian in motive and ideal, in purpose and plan, in attitude and activity. His distinguishing marks are complete honesty with himself, utter sincerity with others, and quiet humility with God. The genuine Christian does not need to defend or protect his religious faith. It is an integral part of him. He does not put it on or take it off like some protective coloration as the occasion demands. It is a permanent possession. He does not lug his faith around with him like some necessary burden. He absorbs it and lives with it.

Sir Alexander Korda, a British film-industry leader, calls Charles Laughton a genius. Describing Mr. Laughton, he said, "He has a feverish will for being superlatively good, a wonderful sincerity." Even critics of the technique of the actor admire his ability to immerse himself in a role, study it, think about it, live it. When he played Rembrandt, he read every scrap he could find about the painter, down to the details of what kind of brushes artists used in the seventeenth century. As the domineering father in *The Barretts of Wimpole Street* he became intolerably high and mighty, even around his own home. When he acted the murderer in *Payment Deferred*, he got so morose he nearly had a nervous breakdown.

This passion for living a part is essential for the real actor. It is much more necessary for the Christian. For he is doing much more than acting a part on a stage. To him has been assigned the role of portraying Christ against the backdrop of an indifferent and evil world. He must study and think and live the part of the Master. He must know the mind of Christ and the meaning of discipleship. His heart must be right with God and his motives in keeping with the Master's will. Only then will the genuineness of his faith be beyond question. "Not every one that saith unto me, Lord, Lord, shall enter into the kingdom of Heaven; but he that doeth the will of my Father which is in heaven."

II

The genuine life *is supported by a common-sense, intelligent faith.* "Not every one that saith unto me, Lord, Lord"—here was a clear warning to the Christians of Jesus' day to beware of making religion a routine and mechanical affair. There were many would-be followers of Jesus who interpreted religion in terms of miracle and magic. To repeat the name itself became a kind of incantation that worked its spell upon the gullible. Worship itself became a racket to prey upon the simple-minded. The people were victimized by clever teachers who used appealing formulas as a substitute for the disciplines of ethical religious training. The early church had many fringe groups that made capital of speaking in tongues and of exorcising devils and healing by rote.

The Master had no use for such a misunderstanding of his message. He made it clear that his was not a religion of wonder working or mystery but that it was a matter of doing the will of God. Indeed, he does not hesitate to call these false teachers of religion "ye that work iniquity."

The strange cults that live like leeches off the main body of the Christian faith are flourishing as strongly today as in the time of Jesus. They make religion look easy. They advertise heavily. They appeal to the credulous. They talk glibly in beautiful abstractions about metaphysical systems, cosmic laws, and the idea of the good. They often conveniently bypass the personal

154

demands of moral character and social responsibility. They promise quick returns in health, wealth, and love. They lift out of context whatever portions of the Bible suit their purpose and ignore the rest of biblical teaching. They are generally critical of the main stream of the Christian faith and church. They sometimes carry on their teaching by mail and solicit money without the accounting of any responsible body. They claim as a rule some special secret vision or revelation of truth that works miracles.

Then there are many fringe groups closer to the Christian church. These include the mercenary, self-appointed evangelists, the so-called faith healers, some professional radio prophets, and many "nonsectarian" store-front missions. These often play on the emotions, parade the spectacular, and prey upon the unwary and uninformed. It is unfortunate but true that there are rack-eteers in religion. There was the case, for instance, of a wandering faith healer from Oklahoma who in Canada caused the death of a young lady who gave up her doctor's insulin treatment for diabetes in the hope of being healed by faith alone.

Within the church, too, there are false prophets who appear in sheep's clothing. They are those who deal in superficial aspects of living or in sensational forms of religious observance, but leave untouched the deep issues of the gospel. They are those who are meticulous in their theological interpretations but who are far from demonstrating the loving spirit of Christ. They are those who insist on their exclusive possession of God's truth and mercy.

Most of us are too polite to criticize another form or view of religion. But Jesus himself was not. He warned against the spurious and unsound quality of any religious expression that exhausts itself in saying, "Lord, Lord," and that does not seek to do the will of God. This was for him the real test of the

validity and genuineness of faith. He called the religious rack-
eteers of his day "wolves in sheep's clothing." Genuine Christians today are not opposed to any man's form of religion. But
they need to remember that there are no easy tricks or short
cuts to mature, serene, and triumphant Christian character and
personality or to a sound Christian society. Christianity is no
panacea. It is a way of life that takes the best of our intelligence
and our strongest will power. The plain fact is that many
Christians do not study and practice their own faith as much
as the cultists. And many likewise are too unwilling to face the
moral demands of the Christian ethic. "Why call ye me, Lord,
Lord, and do not the things which I say?"

Columnist Sydney J. Harris said one time, "We are amused
by novelties, excited by rarities, intrigued by improbabilities.
. . . A two-headed calf is a rarity; but an ordinary calf is a
miracle. A bearded woman is a freak; but a mere woman is a
masterpiece." It is so in religion. Why do men seek the bizarre,
the magical, the freakish, in religious expression in the hope that
it may be more potent? Faith and trust in God as heavenly
Father; acceptance of Jesus Christ and his teaching as the guide
and way of life; concern for our fellow men as brothers in the
family of God's children—these are the heart and soul of the
Christian religion. They are the source and seed of transformed
lives and a changed society. They supply all our needs and command all our powers. They are the basis of the genuine life. For
a genuine life needs the support of a genuine faith, and any
sincere seeker can find in the Christian church all resources and
all varieties of religion without benefit of cultism.

III

The genuine life *bears good fruit*. This is the acid test of a
genuine faith and a genuine life. Speaking of these false teachers

of religion, Jesus says, "Ye shall know them by their fruits. Do men gather grapes of thorns, or figs of thistles? Even so every good tree bringeth forth good fruit; but a corrupt tree bringeth forth evil fruit. A good tree cannot bring forth evil fruit, neither can a corrupt tree bring forth good fruit. . . . Wherefore by their fruits ye shall know them." The same test applies, of course, to any man's religious living. The word "good" used with reference to the tree is better translated "sound." Thus a sound, or genuine, life is known by the quality of its visible product in the form of attitude and action.

This is a hard test for any of us to pass, for in the heat and press of a workaday world the fruitage of our faith tends to spoil.

For instance, many of us tend to become like rotten apples. We look good on the outside, but we are ugly inside. We treat others pleasantly enough to their faces. Behind their backs we hold them in contempt and ridicule. On the surface of our lives we appear clean and sound. Within we are seething with conflicts, impure thoughts, evil intentions. In the showcase we are law-abiding and honest. Behind the counter we display unjust judgments, harsh attitudes, stingy and mean souls.

Then there are the sour grapes—those who limp through life on alibis and excuses. They blame their misfortunes on others or on some dark fate instead of on themselves. They think the world owes them a living and that it is usually against them. They can't enjoy their own lives for looking with envy on the success of others or toward some faraway greener pastures. They make themselves unhappy and then think it is religious to be gloomy. They are grieved because the whole world is out of step with them.

Consider also the green persimmons—those who pucker up and twist all they touch. These people always discount the good works and honest efforts of others with a sneer. They are living question marks, ever doubting real goodness and genuine sincerity. They enjoy a cheap cynicism and are never enthusiastic about any worth-while cause or effort. They delight in finding something wrong and are happiest when criticizing some constructive program, especially of the church. They never believe in anything, even in God, without reservations and loopholes.

Another type of fruit seen in human form is the over-ripe banana—the soft and undependable variety. Such people are discolored with fears and doubts and misgivings. They are the fair-weather Christians, who function as, if, and when it suits their convenience. When the going is rough and sacrifices are called for, they are on the sidelines. They are always willing to concede a principle in order to be socially agreeable or get more business.

Our fruit exhibit would not be complete without the ever-present black walnut. He is a hard nut to crack. He lives deep and safe within himself. He is stolid, unresponsive, hard-boiled, intellectual. He is self-centered, self-opinionated, and just plain selfish. He measures all religion by his own desires and judges all people by his own prejudices.

"Ye shall know them by their fruits." We are shamed by the defective quality of our product! What are the fruits of the Spirit? Paul tells us in Galatians, "The fruit of the Spirit is love, joy, peace, longsuffering, gentleness, goodness, faith, meekness, temperance." These are the tests of any religious teaching. A host of plain Christians are witnesses to these results of their faith. More than this, the fruitful life finds a thousand ways to express its faith. It is eager to help the beaten and oppressed. It is generous in its giving. It is sacrificial in its concern for the causes of humanity and the Kingdom. It seeks ways to lift and lighten the burdens of mankind. It renounces all that is evil and lives to bear witness to the transforming power of God in human life and the beauty and strength of Christian character. It turns defeat into triumph and suffering into joy. Of such is the genuine life! "Not every one that saith unto me, Lord, Lord, shall enter into the kingdom of heaven; but he that doeth the will of my Father which is in heaven."